To Adele and Dolores

THE CHANGING FACE OF FISCAL FEDERALISM

Editors

Thomas R. Swartz
John E. Peck

M. E. SHARPE, INC.
Armonk, New York
London, England

Library of Congress Cataloging-in-Publication Data

The changing face of fiscal federalism / edited by Thomas R. Swartz and
    John E. Peck.
    p. cm.
    ISBN 0-87332-664-4   — ISBN 0-87332-665-2 (pbk.)
    1. Intergovernmental fiscal relations—United States. 2. Fiscal policy—
United States. I. Swartz, Thomas R. II. Peck, John E.
HJ275.C454   1990
336.73—dc20   89-49027
                                                                          CIP

Printed in the United States of America

BB   10   9   8   7   6   5   4   3   2   1

Contents

———— Illustrations ————

Preface

How we share the responsibility for basic government between the federal, state, and local levels has undergone a remarkable change during the past ten years. Over the previous twenty-year period, fiscal responsibility was gradually shifted from lower levels of government to higher levels. Then in 1978 this process was abruptly halted. Under the Carter, the Reagan, and now the Bush administrations, federal support of state and local spending programs was systematically withdrawn. As state governments felt the effects of this federal retrenchment and at the same time suffered the crippling consequences of the 1982–83 recession, they too systematically withdrew their financial support of local governments who were dependent upon them.

The impact of these changes became increasingly apparent: local governments would be expected to shoulder a greater financial burden of providing basic government services in the years ahead. No longer would our cities, towns, school districts, and counties be able to turn to state and federal officials to bail them out. In the words of John Shannon, local governments must learn to "fend for themselves."

What caused this change? How have public policies changed at the federal, state, and local levels of government? What is likely to happen in the future? Who are the winners and who are the losers in this new system of government finance? These are but some of the questions that are considered in this book. In the essays that follow, six of the nation's most highly respected scholars of government finance have placed these issues in appropriate historical context, examined the political and philosophical foundations, analyzed the adjustment process in detail, and peered into the future.

The convening of these scholars and the essays that they produced were made possible by a generous grant from the AT&T Foundation and the active support of the Institute for Scholarship in the Liberal Arts and the Department of Economics at the University of Notre Dame. But it must be noted that the real driving force behind this project was the enthusiastic support of the contributors. They were quick to endorse the concept. Those who visited the campus presented wonderfully stimulating public lectures. Each manuscript was submitted well before our deadlines. And everyone was extraordinarily generous with their time and willingness to provide advice. It can only be concluded that this cooperation and support reflected the importance that the contributors attach to this project.

The publication of this book comes at a critical moment in time. The general public is only now becoming aware of the changes that are occurring around them. This book will help this citizenry make informed judgments as to the advisability of continuing the decentralization of government finance. These political judgments will shape the world we live in as we approach the twenty-first century. As some of our contributors suggest, this could be a radically different world than the one we currently know.

T. R. Swartz
J. E. Peck
1990

THE CHANGING FACE OF FISCAL FEDERALISM

Six Profiles of the Changing Face
of Fiscal Federalism: An Overview

THOMAS R. SWARTZ AND JOHN E. PECK

Overview

A truly remarkable sea change has occurred in how we finance the public
enterprise, yet this change has gone largely unnoticed by the general
public. Policy makers at the federal, state, and local levels of government
have had to respond to this change. Individuals who have suffered its
consequences have had to adjust to a new economic environment. It is
only now, however, that experts in the field of government finance have
begun to chart its future course. The causes of the change, future policy
directions, and the eventual impact on society of this change is the subject
of this book. Six of the nation's most influential economists, political
scientists, and sociologists have been asked to comment on this change.
Their views are found on the pages that follow.

What is this change that is of such concern to these experts? In simple
terms, it is the reshaping of the system of providing basic government
services, and who will pay the bill. In the past ten years, we have reversed
policies that were established by federal lawmakers over the previous thirty
years. What had been a clear and forthright policy to reduce vertical and
horizontal fiscal imbalances among federal, state, and local governments
has given way to the establishment of a new "competitive federalism"
where governments are expected to finance their own activities. That is,
our old system which was characterized by the federal government taking
active steps to level up those governments that did not have the wherewithal
to provide basic government services has been replaced by what John
Shannon calls "fend for yourself federalism"—if a service cannot be paid
for at the level where provided, then do without it.

The implications of operating in a competitive environment are, of
course, the same for governments as they are for individual business

firms. Revenues are revenues, whether raised through taxes or raised through the sale of products. In order to maximize its share of the pie, each governmental unit is required to measure its competition and to implement strategies that lead to survival and, hopefully, to establishing a cushion for future growth. The competitive upside of this policy is a public sector equivalent of Joseph Schumpeter's concept of "creative destruction"—the threat of bankruptcy will force a business enterprise (government) to operate efficiently. They will provide only those goods and services that their constituencies demand and they will provide these goods and services in the most cost-effective manner. Cities, towns, and even states that cannot compete, are simply left behind. Thus the structure of the public sector, like its private sector counterparts, will continually evolve. Those communities that are successful will not only attract new residents and businesses; they will attract imitators who will try to replicate their success. Those that fail will lose population and their economic base. Over time, these communities will simply disappear or learn the harsh lessons of the market and adapt.

The competitive downside is equally clear. When a city, town, or state fails, its elected officials and public workers face the prospect of unemployment, and those residents who are unable to flee must ultimately pay the price for this lack of market efficiency. Government services must be reduced. Taxes must be raised. And the community must brace for its eventual demise, since there is little chance for success under these circumstances. Reduced service levels coupled with higher taxes are certainly not conducive to attracting newcomers or retaining the existing population—particularly if the services that are cut and the taxes that are raised are those affecting the relatively affluent. The question then becomes: who can move and who is forced to stay behind in this competitive environment? Can the less affluent move to the flourishing communities? Can the mom and pop grocery stores leave their neighborhoods? Can the aged be uprooted and moved to new cities and towns? Probably not, since the poor do not have the financial resources to move, the small business units are often dependent upon a local market, and the aged are reluctant to start again in a new and strange place. Thus, when a city, town, or state dies, it traps within it those who cannot move. It traps those who are least able to compete. It traps the poor. It traps the small inefficient firms. It traps the aged.

In these circumstances, it can be argued that the true losers are the citizens who by historic accident happen to reside in less successful jurisdictions. These citizens must now weigh the net benefits of hanging on or of moving on to greener pastures. Critics question whether such a process when applied to the governmental sector is *creative destruction* or merely *destruction*. If it is the latter, it runs counter to the classical notion of *public* service.

This issue above all others is central to *The Changing Face of Fiscal Federalism*. The contributors to this volume are noted authorities on American fiscal federalism. They outline the historic and philosophical foundations of our system of intergovernmental finances. They discuss how responsibilities of the various levels of government are now being sorted out. They consider what new commitments and related costs must be shouldered at each level of government, and they consider how we are likely to pay for the new set of obligations.

Leveling the Playing Field

In 1966, Walter Heller, the principal architect of the fundamental changes in the nation's economic policy under President John F. Kennedy, wrote: "Federal-state-local fiscal relations are at last on the threshold of a *promised land* created by vigorous economic growth and balanced political reapportionment [emphasis added]."[1] With respect to the fiscal implications, Heller referred to his concept of intergovernmental fiscal relations, a system of federal revenue sharing that was both pragmatic and generous. The ideology underlying Heller's optimism—later to be supported by Presidents Johnson and Nixon and finally implemented by Nixon in his policy of "New Federalism"—is best described as a "leveling of the fiscal playing field" for all governmental entities. While virtually every form of grant-in-aid contains an element of generosity on the part of the granting government, some came to view this particular form of sharing as the most generous ever conceived by the federal government, since it avoided the narrowly defined and closely regulated aspects of "categorical" programs. In practice, general revenue sharing, which was put in place in 1972 and finally lifted in 1986, had virtually no strings attached. That is, these federal grants could be used by state and local governments for nearly any purpose they chose.

The revenue sharing idea was first suggested by Henry Clay in the 1820s. It was a part of his "American System"—the basis for the domestic side of the Whig party's program. The first modern bill was introduced by Melvin Laird in the Eisenhower years, but Heller and

Joseph Pechman, on the scene during the Kennedy and Johnson years, were the persons that must be given credit for giving real form to the notion that was finally implemented in 1972.[2] By then, the Advisory Commission on Intergovernmental Relations (ACIR) had dubbed the concept as "an idea whose time has come."[3] The need for leveling up was based on the conviction that in terms of both efficiency and fairness, fiscal federalism should be reshaped to "relieve immediate pressures on state-local treasuries, improve the distribution of federal-state-local fiscal burdens, reduce economic inequalities and fiscal disparities, stimulate state and local tax efforts, and build up the vitality, efficiency, and fiscal independence of state and local governments."[4]

In 1960, before Kennedy's New Frontier, Johnson's Great Society, and Nixon's New Federalism and, therefore, before the notion of leveling up had gained widespread support, there were some one hundred thirty separate *categorical* aid programs which almost exclusively benefited state rather than local governments. These categorical grants were narrowly drawn. The money received could only be spent on the activity that was clearly and concisely specified by the grantor government. Four of the most important categorical grant programs were those that provided employment security, aid to families with dependent children, highway support, and aid to the aged. These four programs alone accounted for 75 percent of total federal grant outlays.

Over the next eighteen years, Congress and the administrations of four presidents had little difficulty adding a number of grant-in-aid programs which by 1978 made up what we know as our system of fiscal federalism. It was the era of new programs: The Economic Opportunity Act, Medicaid, Title I and II of the Elementary and Secondary Education Act, Manpower Training and Development Act, Comprehensive Employment and Training Act, Community Development Block grants, Law Enforcement Assistance Act, and the Economic Development Administration.

President Richard Nixon wrote in his memoirs that the Kennedy and Johnson administrations had erroneously emphasized a centralizing approach to correcting social problems that confront modern industrial countries. He maintained that this "undermined fundamental relationships within our federal system, created confusion about our national values, and corroded American belief in ourselves as a people and as a nation."[5] Nixon's concept of a "New Federalism" was intended to right these wrongs and to reverse the flow of power from the federal government to the states and localities. "The 'New Federalism': revenue sharing, government reorganization, and welfare reform were all directed toward satisfying the national conscience while returning control to the states and localities through a selective decentralization."[6] With the passage of the State and Local Federal Assistance Act of 1972, general revenue sharing became the cornerstone of Nixon's "New Federalism." As with virtually all of the Nixon second term initiatives, the protracted fight for his administration's survival and the eventual fall of his presidency diminished the efficacy of the "New Federalism." Nixon's Special Assistant and an important contributor to the new federalism policy, William Safire, reported of the despair expressed by his administration colleague, George Shultz, for what might have been: "What a waste. In the first term we discovered where the levers were, how to actually change the direction of power away from Washington. . . . Here was a new term, a real mandate, a chance to put some good ideas into action. Now it's all gone up in smoke. We had it in our hands to do such great, sound things, in the way that was right for the country. We had it right in our hands."[7] In dealing with issues of fiscal federalism, President Gerald Ford moved to regain the initiative that the Nixon administration had lost. This new short-lived administration consolidated categorical grant programs into broad block grants. This effort, which allowed state and local governments to spend federal grant monies on a broad array of related programs, represented mid-ground between the unconditional general revenue sharing grants and the narrowly drawn categorical grants. Thus, the Ford effort continued the process of decentralization that was achieved by the general revenue sharing program of 1972, the manpower revenue sharing program of 1973, and the community development block grant program of 1974. The 1976 renewal of general revenue sharing that passed through Congress with Ford's endorsement marked the last fiscal federalism initiative that was introduced during the Ford years.

By the late 1970s, the 130 categorical aid programs of 1960 had given way to more than 500 assistance programs. This financial aid was distributed directly to more than 80 percent of the nation's local governments.[8] Thus, in 1978 the federal government was a major actor in the affairs of state and local governments. Indeed, in 1978, federal aid as a percent of state and local outlays reached its zenith. In that year, more than 25 cents of every dollar spent by lower levels of government was provided by the federal government. This invasion of the federal government into the affairs of state and local governments began to cause widespread concern. Which "piper called the tune"—the federal government that supplied the tax dollars or the state and local governments that spent them? Others worried about the loss of economic efficiency in the system. Would state and local governments be fiscally responsible if they did not generate the tax dollars they spent? Still others were concerned that there were no disincentives for state and local governments to initiate new spending programs. It could be argued, in fact, that the presence of categorical grants would actually encourage these governmental units to adopt new programs, whether they needed them or not. What state or local government could pass up an opportunity to offer its constituency the benefits of a new program if someone else was going to pay the bill?

Competitive Federalism

In retrospect, it is clear that the years from 1960 to 1978 were the "golden years" of fiscal federalism for state and local governments. Many of these governments began the period with severe fiscal stress: there was rural poverty in Appalachia, the urban poverty particularly in the older cities of the Northeast and Great Lakes states, and lagging economies found in the "old South." Nearly all of these regions and cities emerged at the end of the "golden years" well on the way to financial health. Budget surpluses were commonplace. The impact of the Kennedy/Johnson Appalachian Programs was realized at the same time as energy prices rose in the face of OPEC's efforts to squeeze oil supplies. This coincidence of events caused the once idle coal region to find a new life. The worst of the urban blight disappeared and some of the most distressed cities began to experience a renaissance. Lastly, the South began to stir. President Johnson moved the space industry southward, and soon other industries followed suit as they left the snowbelt in search of the now air-conditioned South and Southwest.

America seemed to have turned a corner. The need to level the playing field was less obvious. Perhaps we thought that the problems of the poor were solved when we no longer saw the rawest, meanest side of poverty, and the physical decay of our cities was largely eliminated. Or, we believed that the devastating consequences of racism were behind us when steps were finally taken to integrate the public schools. Or, we trusted that all cities were financially secure once the near financial collapse of some major urban places such as New York, Cleveland, and Newark was averted. Whatever the cause, we began to act as if our cities, towns, and states could go it alone and pay their own way.

Our national mood suddenly changed in the late 1970s. To be more precise about this, our national mood began to change on the morning of June 7, 1978. That was the morning when Californians went to the polls and passed Proposition 13 (the Jarvis-Gunn Amendment). This 389-word amendment to the California State Constitution set in motion a radical shift in our system of fiscal federalism. In one bold stroke, it reduced the most important source of local government tax revenues, the property tax, by 57 percent and saved local California taxpayers nearly seven billion dollars per year. It established a property tax rate limit of 1 percent for all real property—that is, the nominal property tax rate applied to all homes, farms, factories, businesses, and vacant lots. It rolled the 1978 assessment levels back to amounts that existed in 1975–76[9] and froze them at that level until the property was sold or improved. It limited future yearly increases in individual property tax bills to a maximum of 2 percent per year, and mandated that the state legislature obtain a two-thirds majority of both houses if it were to increase any other tax in California.

Within months of the passage of Proposition 13, numerous states followed the California lead by placing tax/expenditure control referenda before their voters. The airwaves and the print media were filled with news of Michigan's Headlee Amendment, Massachusetts' Proposition 2½, Florida's Proposition 1, and Howard Jarvis, the principal architect of Proposition 13, launched a nationwide crusade to bring new control legislation into being in every state and local government across the country. In the first three years after enactment of Proposition 13, twenty-two states placed fifty-one new fiscal controls on their counties, cities, and school corporations. A vast majority of these, thirty-five out of fifty-one, were aimed at limiting local government fiscal discretion. Some of these restrictions limited the tax rate that could be applied to assessed value, others imposed a ceiling on the property tax levies, some placed controls on the assessment of property, and still others mandated that a taxpayer's property tax liability be fully explained so that they would know exactly how they were being taxed and how large their tax liability was. (The intention of this legislation was clear. If a taxpayer knew the extent of tax liability, then he or she would be inclined to fight future tax increases.) In addition to these explicit property tax controls, a number of states limited the total tax collections of their local governments. And, in a spirit of introspection, sixteen states placed controls on their own taxing and/or spending powers.

The fiscal controls that states rushed to place upon local governments and themselves were not the only legacies of Proposition 13. The mood of fiscal conservatism spread to the federal level as more and more states turned to limitation schemes. That is, federal policy makers began to sense the shift in public opinion and they in turn began to adopt more fiscally conservative positions. Ironically, as the essays in this book detail, the federal government's fiscal conservatism resulted in a systematic reduction in the support of state and local government programs, which forced state governments to abandon their tax and spending control initiatives. The combined effect of federal action coupled with state reaction resulted in even more lasting and important implications for the present course of fiscal federalism.

In the face of wrenching policy changes, perceived traditional political lines became blurred. As early as 1978, Democrats joined Republicans in a call for a reexamination of the growth of domestic spending programs. This reexamination was broad based and included some previously thought to be sacred cows, such as revenue sharing, entitlements, and the pass-alongs that had grown with such ferocity in the decades before. While the image of David Stockman wading through government programs with a long, curved scythe was a familiar one, the grinning Jimmy Carter was responsible for taking the scythe out of the barn. President Carter called his budget for fiscal year 1980 ''lean and austere.'' He recommended that the rate of increase in government spending be slowed so that it would break the ''momentum'' of federal spending. He recognized that this reversal in public policy would ''disappoint'' many of his supporters, but he argued that the tenor of the times made it impolitic to continue to increase ''Federal efforts across the board.''[10]

By the time budget deliberations had begun for fiscal year 1980, general revenue sharing had become one of Carter's prime targets. He proposed to renew the program, but to renew it for the benefit of local governments alone. State allotments were to be abandoned. This, of course, reduced the available funds that states could pass along as local allotments. In response to Carter's budget request, Congress passed a modified general revenue sharing program aimed solely at local governments incorporating a current dollar reduction of 25 percent. Unfortunately for local governments, President Carter's budgeted cuts were not limited to general revenue sharing. He pushed for reductions in grants for local public works projects, public service employment, and countercyclical revenue sharing. The overall implication was clear. After eighteen years of "leveling up," the federal government, faced with its own monumental problems—a soaring operational budget and yearly deficits that some felt were out of control—would no longer underwrite a larger and larger share of state and local expenditures. At this point, Heller's dream of a "promised land" began to fade. It proved to be an elusive target, and for some it was no target at all.

The impact of Carter's "lean and austere" budgets on our system of fiscal federalism paled in comparison with what was to follow. Ronald Reagan dramatically changed the direction and the thrust of how we have come to share the burden of providing basic governmental services. His was a vision of yet another kind of "New Federalism." George Peterson of the Urban Institute's Public Finance Center wrote in 1984 of the Reagan ideological change: "Ronald Reagan is the first president since Franklin D. Roosevelt to challenge not just the workings of the intergovernmental system but the prevailing ideology of his time. His alternative vision of federalism can be summarized in three phrases: 'separation of powers,' 'devolution of responsibilities to governments that are closer to the people,' and 'less spending by all levels of government.' Each has powerful antecedents in conservative thought."[11]

This new president did not waffle. He made his intentions clear to all. In his Inaugural Address, he let it be known that he would "curb the size and influence of the federal establishment" and that he would throw the full weight of his office behind efforts to reestablish "the distinction between the powers granted to the federal government, [and] those reserved to the states or to the people."[12] While some might debate whether or not "the people" are better represented by local government than they are by the federal or state governments, there was no doubt where Reagan stood on the issue. He effectively championed the notion that local government was closest to the people and, therefore, local policy makers were more likely to interpret the preferences of a community than their counterparts in state capitols or those who were isolated in the District of Columbia. Given the opportunity, Reagan would choose to assign local taxpayers the authority to decide which national programs they would support, how much they would spend, and how they would control the implementation at the local level. [13]

Operationally, Reagan's "New Federalism" would make major changes in the existing system of intergovernmental finance, a system which he believed was poorly conceived and out of control. Carter's cuts in federal spending were large and meaningful, but they were associated more with a reduction of antirecession policies than with a fundamental reversal in the course of government finance.

In his 1982 State of the Union message, Reagan outlined a ten-year program that would realign program responsibilities in the federal/state partnership—responsibility for Aid to Families with Dependent Children and the Food Stamp program would be shifted to the states, while Medicaid would become the sole responsibility of the federal government. The administrative responsibility of sixty-one additional programs of less important impact would also be transferred to state governments to be temporarily funded by a federal trust fund backed by excise taxes on alcohol, tobacco, telephones, and motor fuels. After five years, the trust fund was to be dissolved and the states would have to raise their own funds to continue the programs. ''If consummated in full, the New Federalism would have severed intergovernmental ties to such an extent that, by 1991, the grant-in-aid share of the state and local budgets would have fallen to 3 to 4 percent, the lowest level since the first year of the New Deal.''[14]

While the Reagan years were marked by substantial shifts from the nondefense budgets to the defense budgets, the announced program of New Federalism and its underlying reorganization of governmental responsibilities was never broadly accepted by federal lawmakers, taxpayers, or the states themselves. Nevertheless, termination of general revenue sharing in 1986, and deep cuts in state-local grants-in-aid, food stamps, programs designed to protect the environment and natural resources, farm supports, and in a host of other programs ranging from veterans' benefits to trade adjustment assistance had both direct and indirect effects upon state and local finances. The direct loss or reduction of federal funding in many of these program areas was simply not matched by a reduction in demand for the services that they supported. This was particularly true in periods of economic stress like the recession of 1982–83. Accordingly, many states were forced to assume the financial burden of these programs. If they did not have the fiscal capacity to take on these responsibilities, they were forced to reduce services.

The changes that began with Proposition 13, then, had come full circle. The tax relief and reduction measures of the late 1970s began to give way to a round of new state tax increases. That is, as the federal programs began to disappear, states had to fend for themselves. Thirty-four states increased taxes in 1981, twenty-five legislated increases in 1982, and, as the full force of the 1982–83 recession became evident, forty-one had to raise at least one of their taxes in 1983. While the first wave of tax increases were weighted heavily toward "nuisance" taxes, as the severity of the revenue gap became more obvious, state governments were forced to turn to their broad-based sales and income taxes for fiscal relief.

The irony, of course, is that although Reagan's formal program of realigning fiscal responsibilities for basic government programs was rejected by Congress, the thrust of his "New Federalism" was, in fact, put in place. Thus, as we approach the end of the 1980s, Reagan's "New Federalism" has become a reality.

It should be emphasized that the real burden of the shifts has been reserved for local governments. The impact on these governmental units was compounded. At the same time that the federal government was withdrawing from participating directly in state and local expenditure programs, the states began to withdraw from participating in purely local expenditure programs. Total state aid as a percentage of local government revenues fell from more than 63 percent in 1980 to less than 55 percent in 1987. Local governments, particularly county and city governments, were far more dependent upon their own sources of revenue, which in most cases translated into greater dependence upon the local property tax. The spirit of Proposition 13 was turned on its head in the matter of a few short years. In practical terms, however, where legislated property tax controls remained, local governments found themselves squeezed from both ends—both internal and external traditional sources of funds were increasingly restricted.

The contrast between the Nixon and Reagan concepts of "New Federalism" was clear. While both policies were based upon the desirability of moving program responsibility closer to the individual taxpayer, Nixon intended that the federal government would share in program costs while Reagan aimed to decentralize the full fiscal responsibility as well.

If, then, states—and therefore local governments—are to share an increasing portion of the costs associated with providing basic governmental services, it will naturally follow that some taxing jurisdictions will encounter severe difficulties in meeting these responsibilities. One underlying purpose of the old system of fiscal federalism was to recognize and compensate for differences in the fiscal capabilities of certain state and local governments. Since this purpose has been abandoned, state and local governments are increasingly free to operate on their own in a system of "competitive federalism."

Thus, one of the most significant changes in government finance has occurred as a "quiet revolution." It started with the fanfare of California's Proposition 13—hailed as a tax revolt by those who believed that government had grown too large—but in three short years, many states that had enacted controls were forced to retreat from their strong stances. Another more subtle revolution was underway. With little congressional debate and even less public awareness, we had changed—for better or worse—how we would provide for the public good. This is the legacy of Ronald Reagan's presidency—a legacy that is likely to be with us for many years to come.

Six Profiles of the Changing Face of Fiscal Federalism

A number of questions are yet to be resolved. What is in store for state and local governments in both the near and long term? Can program responsibility be systematically sorted out by level of government in the present environment? What are the costs of these changes and who will bear the burden? These are some of the issues that are addressed in the essays that follow. In the initial essay entitled "The Deregulation of the American Federal System: 1789–1989," John Shannon, who for many years served as the executive director of the Advisory Commission on Intergovernmental Relations and who now serves as a senior fellow at the Urban Institute, traces the constitutional roots and the two hundred year history of how we divide up the responsibility of providing basic government goods and services. Shannon isolates three periods: Constitutional Federalism (1789–1929); Crisis Federalism (1929–53); and Fiscal Federalism (1953 to present). The focus of his essay is upon the latter period, since it is here that we see the swift rise in federal participation and its equally swift retreat. Shannon offers reasons for the policy reversal and looks optimistically to the future.

The second essay, penned by Richard Child Hill of Michigan State University is entitled "Federalism and Urban Policy: The Intergovernmental Dialectic." Hill concentrates on what Shannon identified as the third phase, "fiscal federalism," and provides an alternative explanation for the rise and fall of federal support of state/local programs. In Hill's view, we have experienced a shift away from a social welfare based policy to a public policy of economic growth. Like Shannon, he offers a compelling rationale for the change in policy but, unlike Shannon, he is less optimistic about the future consequences of the change.

Roy Bahl, the longtime director of the Metropolitan Studies Program at the Maxwell School, Syracuse University, and currently director of the Policy Research Program at Georgia State University, provides the third essay. His paper is simply titled ''Changing Federalism: Trends and Interstate Variations.'' Bahl's work is the first of four papers that examine in detail the adjustment process that has taken place since policy changed in 1978. He begins his essay by chronicling the growth in state/local spending and the role played by the federal government in this growth. He then attempts to explain the sharp interstate variations he uncovers, to determine whether the fiscal condition of some state and local governments has been compromised by the demands placed upon them, and to examine fiscal federalism under the Bush administration.

Steven D. Gold, director of Fiscal Studies for the National Conference of State Legislatures, gives us even more detail as to how state governments have conformed to what he calls the ''New Era of Fiscal Federalism.'' Gold warns his readers that the changes that have occurred cannot be viewed in isolation, rather they must be interpreted in a broad, historic context that attempts to take into account the wide variety of changes that impact federal, state, and local governments. To this end, he reviews state tax and spending policy before and after 1978 and examines the fiscal condition of states in light of the federal cutbacks. Gold then goes on to analyze the single most important expenditure responsibility of state governments, education. In the end, he finds that although the future is not bright, the consequences of the change are often exaggerated for state governments. They will, however, need to muster all of their resources to meet the impending fiscal challenges.

These conclusions do not bode well for local governments that are dependent upon the largess of their state governments. This concern is the subject of our fifth essay by Helen F. Ladd, the director of Graduate Studies and professor in the Institute of Policy Sciences and Public Affairs at Duke University. Ladd disagrees with those who conclude that cities have weathered the changes quite well and that, by the mid-1980s, they were in a relatively strong fiscal position. She finds that the improvement in their financial condition has been modest. More importantly, she finds that there are serious questions about the underlying fiscal health of our large cities. Over time, this financial health has deteriorated and many will need additional state and federal assistance in order to provide adequate public services at reasonable tax rates.

Edward M. Gramlich of the University of Michigan grapples with the

"Economics of Fiscal Federalism" in the concluding essay of the volume. Gramlich develops the broad outlines of an ideal system of fiscal federalism. He then compares a normative model of what should ideally happen with the nation's current structure of fiscal federalism. His examination of both expenditures and taxes suggests that the system is generally working quite well; however, he finds exceptions to that conclusion and offers some reforms designed to improve equity, efficiency, and even reduce the size of the federal deficit. Thus, the Gramlich essay leaves us with a rationale for the sorting out process by considering the inevitable need to assign expenditure and tax responsibilities.

The overall contribution of the book, then, is to provide a review, an appraisal, and an outlook of the evolving new system of fiscal federalism—a new federalism whose time has not only come, but is upon us in full force. A new federalism that will affect the lives of each and every one of us.

Notes

1. Walter W. Heller, *New Dimensions of Political Economy* (Cambridge: Harvard University Press, 1966), p. 117.

2. A. James Reichley, *Conservatives in an Age of Change* (Washington, DC: The Brookings Institution, 1981), pp. 154–55.

3. Advisory Commission on Intergovernmental Relations, *Federal Revenue Sharing: A Report* (Washington, DC: USGPO, 1974).

4. Heller, *New Dimensions of Political Economy*, p. 144.

5. Richard Nixon, *RN: The Memoirs of Richard Nixon* (New York: Grosset and Dunlap, 1978), p. 352.

6. William Safire, *Before the Fall* (Garden City, NY: Doubleday and Company, 1975), p. 463.

7. Ibid., p. 231.

8. Advisory Commission on Intergovernmental Relations, *An Agenda for American Federalism: Restoring Confidence and Competence* (Washington, DC: USGPO, June 1981), pp. 1–6.

9. California reassessed all real property on an annual basis prior to the passage of Proposition 13.

10. President Jimmy Carter, State of the Union Address, 1978.

11. George E. Peterson, "Federalism and the States," in *The Reagan Record*, John L. Palmer and Isabel V. Sawhill, eds. (Cambridge, MA: Ballinger Publishing Company, 1984), pp. 222–23.

12. President Ronald Reagan, Inaugural Address, January 20, 1981.

13. Peterson, "Federalism and the States," pp. 223–24.

14. Palmer and Sawhill, *The Reagan Record*, p. 220.

— 2 —

The Deregulation of the American Federal System: 1789–1989

JOHN SHANNON

Shortly after the end of World War II, George Orwell painted a bleak future for modern democracy: he warned that by 1984 the central government ("Big Brother") could become all powerful and individual freedom a thing of the past. In less gloomy terms, students of American federalism also made their predictions after World War II. Many agreed that the state governments were the "fallen arches" of our federal structure and viewed the centralization of power in Washington as inevitable if not desirable.

When attempting to ascertain where we are going, looking back over the shoulder often proves more instructive than simply using current events as the predictors of things to come. So as better to judge the current condition and future course of our federal system, the year 1989 is staked out in this paper as the high vantage point from which to look back and examine the major changes in the relationship between the federal government and the state-local systems since George Washington first assumed the presidency in 1789.

Tracing the great changes in the relationship between Washington and the state-local systems over the last two hundred years, however, provides only part of the picture of the American federal system. Contemporary federalism is marked by fiscal diversity, intergovernmental competitiveness, and state-local resiliency—three significant features that also require highlighting.

Constitutional Federalism: 1789–1929

For one hundred forty years, the continued presence of a very small federal government provided conclusive evidence of the enduring effectiveness of constitutional constraints when strongly backed by the force of public opinion. As late as 1929, total federal spending amounted to 2.5 percent of GNP—about one-third the amount raised and spent that year by the states and local governments.

This constitutional constraint system rested on the principle that the national government's jurisdictional reach should remain highly restricted—exercising only those powers delegated to it by the U.S. Constitution. To nail down this limited government concept, the founders added the Tenth Amendment to the Constitution: it stipulates that all powers not delegated to the federal government were reserved for the states and the people.

Public opinion powerfully reinforced this limited government principle. From the time that George Washington took the oath of office in 1789 to the stock market crash of 1929, most Americans clearly favored small government in general and a very small federal domestic presence in particular. This tradition of self-reliance shaped congressional and judicial behavior. In determining how far the federal government should venture out into the domestic sector—largely the state-local domain—both Congress and the federal courts generally resolved the doubts in favor of a fairly strict (restrictive) construction of their delegated powers, especially the national spending power.

In retrospect, this strict construction/limited national government era becomes all the more remarkable when viewed against an historical backdrop marked by great crises and social change—the ordeal of the Civil War, the waging of four other wars, the winning of the West, the shock of several economic panics, the growing industrialization of an agrarian economy, and finally the emergence of the United States as a leading world power in the early twentieth century.

Using a narrow interpretation of the national government's powers also facilitated a fairly clear division of intergovernmental labor. While the federal and state-local sectors never operated in separate, airtight compartments, the states and their local governments supplied most of the domestic governmental needs of a society marked by a very modest taste for public goods and services. In contrast, Washington confined its activities primarily to four major national concerns—the defense of the union against internal and external threats, the retirement of large debts incurred in wartime, the winning of the West, and the promotion of the common market interests of a steadily growing free enterprise economy.

With his succinct observation that "the business of America is business," President Calvin Coolidge both captured the spirit of this 140 year era of limited national government and reaffirmed the probusiness strategy of that formidable federalist, Alexander Hamilton.

Crisis Federalism: 1929–53

Between 1929 and the end of the Korean War in 1953, a series of crises profoundly changed the political and judicial thinking about the proper size of the public sector in general and the size and role of the federal sector in particular. These attitudinal changes, in turn, pushed aside the traditional constitutional barriers to federal entry into areas that had previously been viewed as either the exclusive preserve of the states or the natural domain of the private sector.

The Great Depression

The stock market crash of 1929 set in motion economic forces that hastened the collapse of Constitutional Federalism. The fall of the old constitutional regime was accomplished by undercutting its three major props: the judicial prop—a highly restrictive construction of federal power; the economic prop—a laissez faire policy; and the political prop—a very small federal domestic presence.

A searing national crisis—the Great Depression—left in its wake an unprecedented number of unemployed persons, bank failures, business bankruptcies, and farm and home foreclosures. These rapidly mounting economic and social casualties quickly overwhelmed the resources of the private and state-local sectors. They also triggered a strident political demand for help from Washington.

First the Congress and later the U.S. Supreme Court acceded to the Roosevelt administration's call for a New Deal—an unprecedented use of national government power to overhaul and jump-start a badly stalled economy. Because New Deal economic reforms went far beyond the traditional constitutional view of the acceptable limits, the Supreme Court declared unconstitutional several pioneering efforts—the National Industrial Recovery Act, the Guffey Snyder Act of 1935, and the Agricultural Adjustment Act.

Strong and hostile political reaction to the Supreme Court's strict construction policy had its intended effects. In the famous "switch in time that saved nine," the Court began in 1937 to take a far broader view of the national government's powers, thus placing its judicial imprimatur on Crisis Federalism in general and on the New Deal Revolution in particular. Between 1937 and 1942, the Court upheld the federal government's right to regulate agriculture output, to supervise labor-industrial relations, to shape regional development (Tennessee Valley Authority—TVA), and to provide social security and unemployment compensation benefits.

By 1942, the nation had witnessed the virtual disappearance of the once powerful constraints on federal regulation of the economy. Gone also were the time-honored concepts of Dual Federalism and limited national government.

The Three War Crises: 1941–53

While the forces of the Great Depression swept away most of the legal and political barriers to federal activism, the bunching of three war crises—first, World War II, then the emergence of the Cold War, and finally the Korean War—enormously strengthened and solidified the fiscal power of the national government. Expenditures for national defense which amounted to only one percent of GNP just prior to World War II ballooned to 12 percent of GNP by the end of the Korean War. While relying heavily on the sale of war bonds to help finance World War II, Congress powerfully strengthened its two primary tax producers—the corporate and individual income taxes.

The transformation of the individual income tax stands out as an especially significant development for our federal system. By radically increasing tax rates, sharply cutting personal exemptions and even more important—introducing income tax withholding in 1943—Congress converted a "rich man's tax" into an "everyman's tax." Although there were a couple of tax rate cuts between the end of World War II and the outbreak of the Korean War, they were relatively modest because the congressional urge to cut high tax rates was held in check by the need both to retire war debt and to face up to the realities of the emerging Cold War. Thus, when the Korean War broke out in 1950 the income tax was still a powerful revenue producer. By raising tax rates to record highs, Congress was then able to put the financing of the Korean War largely on a pay-as-we-fight basis. In retrospect, World War II and the Korean War combined to create the most productive revenue producer in the history of mankind: the federal individual income tax.

To sum up, the era of Crisis Federalism—1929 to 1953—must stand out as the truly revolutionary period in the two hundred year history of American federalism. The explosive growth of the national government is most sharply underscored by one startling statistic. At the beginning of this crisis-ridden period in 1929, federal spending amounted to 2.5 percent of GNP—only a third of the outlays of the state-local sector. By the end of the Korean War in 1953, total federal spending had soared to 19 percent of GNP—an amount two and a half times greater than total state-local outlays (Exhibit 2.1). In this quarter of a century, the federal government had risen in status from that of one among several world powers to that of the undisputed leader of the Free World. In this same twenty-five year period, the federal government had sprung up in jack-and-the-beanstalk-fashion to tower over the state-local landscape.

As Crisis Federalism drew to a close, it is also necessary to clarify the new federal relationship to the state-local systems. The crucial point is this: Washington did not come even close to assuming control of the states and their localities despite the fact that (a) in fiscal terms, it now towered over them, and (b) its influence over the state-local sector had definitely grown with the rise in federal aid. Why not control? Because states and local governments still retained primary responsibility for both the financing and the delivery of most of the basic services identified with the domestic public sector—the maintenance of law and order, the education of the youth, the regulation of domestic relations and many business relationships, the protection of public health, the control of land use, and the provision of local public amenities (libraries, parks, and museums). In short, the federal sector had grown enormously but the state-local sector did not shrivel.

It is also important to note the "laboratory" character of American federalism. During the Great Depression crisis, Washington policy makers drew heavily on the innovative and pioneering experiences of certain liberal states (e.g., Wisconsin and New York) when drafting some of their most important pieces of New Deal social welfare legislation—unemployment compensation and certain other social security-type reforms.

Fiscal Federalism: 1953 to Present

With the collapse of the constitutional and political constraints, the strength or the weakness of the fiscal constraint has become the single most important factor governing the expansion or the contraction of federal influence over the state-local sector. Just as Constitutional Fed-

Exhibit 2.1. Fiscal Federalism: The Rise and Decline of Federal Aid, 1958–88 (as a percentage of state-local outlays)

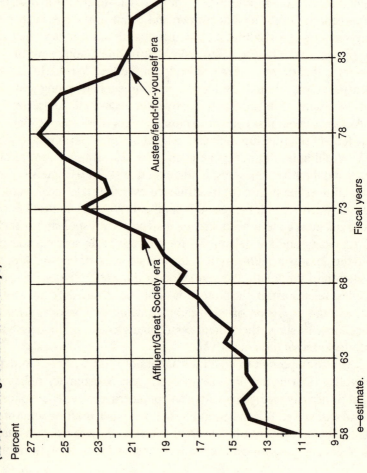

Percent

Fiscal years

e—estimate.

Source: ACIR Staff.

eralism gave way to Crisis Federalism, so it, in turn, gave way to Fiscal Federalism.

To be more specific, the status of the federal budget now largely shapes the character of the general relationship between Washington and the state-local systems. When Congress finds itself in an "easy" budget situation, additional federal aid dollars (with expenditure strings attached) flow into the state-local sector at a faster rate than do additional dollars from state and local sources. Thus as federal aid becomes a progressively larger share of state and local budgets, federal influence over the state-local sector expands. Conversely, in a period marked by many years of "tight" federal budgets, federal aid becomes a progressively smaller fraction of state and local budgets and, as a result, federal influence on state and local policy makers tends to decline although not as rapidly as the fall-off in federal aid. Why? Because federal expenditure strings are "stickier" than the federal aid dollars that accompany them.

Federal Aid: Its Rise and Decline

The expansive phase of federal influence began with the end of the Korean War and crested in 1978 marking the high tide of federal aid to states and localities (Exhibit 2.2). During this twenty-five year period, there was an explosive growth in the number of federal aid programs, which soared from thirty-eight programs in 1954 to almost five hundred aid programs by 1978. During most of these years, federal aid also grew at a faster pace than did state-local revenue. As a result, federal aid grew steadily from 10 percent of state-local expenditures in 1953 to 26 percent by 1978. This federal aid growth becomes even more remarkable when it is recalled that state and local revenues were growing at a consistently faster rate than the economy.

If this expansive period can be labelled the "Easy" Federal Budget Era of fiscal federalism, it was followed by a striking reversal—the emergence of the Tight Federal Budget Era. Since 1978 and continuing to the present, two forces—growing federal budget difficulties and strong public support for President Reagan's conservative and decentralist policies—combined to cause a real decline in federal aid flows. As a percentage of state-local outlays, federal aid has fallen steadily from 26 percent in 1978 to an estimated 17 percent by 1988. This federal aid decline takes on added significance because in real terms state-local own source revenue has risen quite slowly in the post–Proposition 13 era.

Exhibit 2.2. Crisis Federalism: Explosive Growth of Federal Government, 1929–54 (expenditures as a percentage of gross national product)

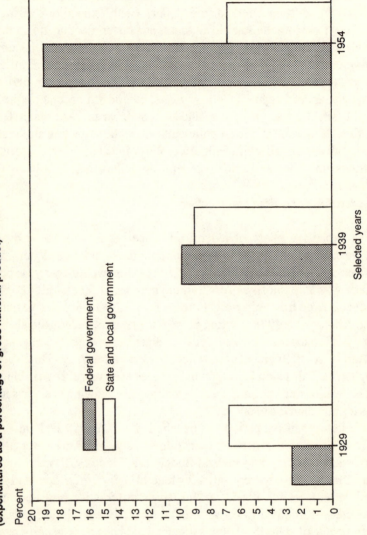

Percent

Federal government

State and local government

1929

1939

1954

Selected years

Source: ACIR staff, *Significant Features of Fiscal Federalism 1987*, Table 1.

Expansion and Contraction: Primary Factors

In retrospect, the 1953–78 period will probably go down in history as the golden fiscal era for the national government—a period in which Washington could cut personal income taxes time and again while more than doubling its presence on the domestic sector front. During this quarter of a century, federal domestic programs (including the aid to state and local governments) rose from about 6 percent to 15 percent of Gross National Product.

This great federal surge is especially noteworthy when it is recalled that state and local revenues grew far more slowly, despite the fact that states and localities were doing a very good business in new and used taxes. Moreover, in sharp contrast to the relatively tranquil federal experience, the path to stronger state and local revenue systems was paved with the political bones of many elected state and local officials. No wonder representatives of the state governments pointed out this fiscal imbalance and urged federal revenue sharing as the way to correct the mismatch.

This fiscal imbalance situation raises the basic question: Why could federal policy makers move so much further, faster, and more safely than could state and local officials into the domestic public sector—an area that traditionally had been of primary concern to state and local policy makers? Part of the answer is fiscal. Federal officials came out of Crisis Federalism holding several fiscal trump cards—easy money sources—which enabled them to expand rapidly on the domestic front at little political risk. Part of the answer is nonfiscal. The Cold War provided Washington with the national defense rationale it needed to push through the interstate highway and education grants in the 1950s and the Civil Rights Revolution gave the Great Society programs a powerful push in the 1960s.

The Income Tax Trump Card

As noted earlier, the federal government came out of the World War II and the Korean War crises with a massive income tax. During most of the 1953–78 period, the interaction of economic growth and inflation with the progressive income tax rate structure produced sufficient additional tax revenue to help finance repeated tax cuts and at the same time expand federal domestic programs.

While federal policy makers still hold a valuable income tax card, it can no longer be played with the same flourish that characterized its play in the 1960s and early 1970s. Indexation and a much flatter tax-rate structure have taken most of automatic growth out of the income tax sails.

Defense Trump Card

The United States also came out of Korea with a heavy defense commitment, spending almost twice as many dollars on defense related programs as did all states and localities for all their programs combined. Between the end of the Korean War and 1978, defense-related outlays steadily dropped from about 12 to 4.5 percent of GNP. Part of this great drop in defense spending was used to finance tax cuts but much of it went to underwrite the shift from defense to nondefense spending. No governor or mayor had such a fiscal fountain of youth—a financing source that permitted Congress to expand federal domestic spending while cutting federal taxes.

The Russian invasion of Afghanistan in 1979 put an end to this fiscal trump card as defense outlays started on their upward course during the second half of the Carter administration. The Reagan administration quickly strengthened this defense build-up, with outlays for the Pentagon reaching 6.5 percent of GNP, by the middle 1980s.

The Budget Deficit Trump Card

During this golden era (1953–78), deficit financing became quite respectable. In twenty-two of the twenty-five fiscal years, federal policy makers covered revenue shortfalls with the issuance of bonded indebtedness thereby avoiding the political pain associated with program cuts or tax hikes.

The 1980s proved that quantitative differences in deficits can have qualitative differences in policy outcomes. During the Reagan administration, budget deficits became so massive that the public could no longer ignore them. The business community and especially foreign investors now regard the chronic presence of large U.S. deficits as having a destabilizing effect on both the national and world economies. Thus, where once deficit financing provided another easy source of additional funding for federal spenders, now the need to reduce budget deficits and balance the budget has powerfully strengthened the hands of the fiscal conservatives.

In determining the expansion or contraction of federal aid flows, the presence or the absence of easy money sources is a more important factor than the presence or absence of a Democrat in the White House. The expansion of federal aid during the easy budget era (1953–78) continued under both Democratic and Republican administrations because Washington policy makers had access to certain easy sources of financing— fiscal trump cards—not available to state and local officials. The contraction of federal aid and influence began in the mid-term of the Carter administration when it became apparent that Washington could no longer keep pumping an ever increasing share of its resources into the state-local sector. The elimination of the state component of revenue sharing and the antirecession financial assistance grants signaled the end of the golden era and the beginning of federal aid pull-back on the state-local front.

The Reagan administration hurried this retrenchment history along by accelerating the defense build-up and engineering a major tax cut—actions that created massive federal budget deficits and forced states and localities to become more self-reliant. In this era of tightening federal budget constraints, fend-for-yourself federalism emerged as the guiding principle shaping Washington's relationship with the states and localities.

A Sorting Out of Sorts

The gradual decentralization process outlined above is not the neat, orderly, and swift sorting-out process for which reformers yearn. Nor does it resemble the program swap and tax turnback proposals the Reagan administration advanced in 1982 for achieving a more orderly and decentralized allocation of responsibilities between the national government and the fifty state-local systems.

Nevertheless, fend-for-yourself federalism is slowly effecting a "sorting out" of sorts. Federal policy makers are being forced by fiscal and political realities to allocate an increasing share of their resources for strictly national government programs: defense, social security, Medicare, and interest on a $3 trillion debt. To sum up, three significant changes have emerged from the interaction of the federal budget crisis and the Reagan decentralist philosophy:

• A sea change has occurred in the expectations of state and local officials: when forced to search for "new money," they once again look to their own resources.

• The recent burst in state activism and the remarkable demonstration of state-local fiscal resiliency can be attributed in no small part to this return to fend-for-yourself federalism.

• Federalists no longer worry that states and localities will become "federal aid junkies."

Contemporary Federalism: Three Significant Features

In addition to Washington's fend-for-yourself relationship with the states and localities, contemporary federalism is marked by fiscal diversity, intergovernmental competitiveness, and state-local resiliency.

Diversity—Providing Choices

Because all states and most localities must raise most of their revenue, there are great variations in state and local tax and expenditure policies in the United States. These fiscal differences—which provide real choices for citizens and business firms—are found in all regions of the country:

In New England: New Hampshire has neither a broad-based personal income tax nor a general sales tax, and leans heavily, therefore, on the local property tax. The neighboring states make use of all three of these revenue producers.

In the Mid-Atlantic Region: State and local expenditures (per capita) for New York are far above average, while Pennsylvania's expenditures are definitely below the national average.

In the Great Lakes Region: There is a real difference between the progressive tax policies of Minnesota and Wisconsin and those of the more conservative states of Illinois and Indiana.

In the Far West: An interesting choice exists between Washington State, where voters have repeatedly voted down an income tax, and Oregon, where voters are strongly opposed to a sales tax.

A Striking Interregional Difference: New England states make above average use of the property tax and place heavy emphasis on local control. In contrast, southern states make rather sparing use of the property tax and favor more centralized state financing. These great differences can be traced largely to three factors: (a) widespread variations in fiscal capacity, (b) substantial differences in voters' tastes for both public services and taxes to support them, and (c) a federal hands-off tradition with respect to equalizing intergovernmental fiscal disparities.

These great state and local fiscal variations are viewed quite differently by liberals and conservatives. Liberals often view such fiscal differences as disparities, and call for equalizing federal and state actions. Most conservatives tend to view the variations as diversities that should not be wiped out by redistributive federal and state actions. For the supporters of decentralized government, one of the toughest policy issues is this: When does a "good diversity" become a "bad disparity" that necessitates corrective federal and/or state action?

However one views these variations, one thing is clear: state and local boundaries do make a difference in the American federal system. In the United States, "You pays your money and you takes your choice."

Competitiveness—Stabilizing the System

If diversity is one of the hallmarks of American fiscal federalism, what prevents our fifty state-local systems from becoming too diverse? Again, the quick answer: Competition for jobs and economic development appears to be an important factor in preventing our states from drifting too far apart.

The fifty state-local systems behave much like ships in a naval convoy in wartime. Because they are spread out over a great area, there is considerable room for each state to maneuver within the convoy. Two considerations prevent a state from moving out too far ahead or lagging too far behind.

1. If a state moves out too far ahead of the convoy on the tax side, it becomes increasingly vulnerable to tax evasion, taxpayer revolts and, most importantly, to tax competition for jobs and investments from other states.

2. If a state-local system lags too far behind the convoy on the public service side, it becomes increasingly vulnerable to quality of life and economic development concerns: poor schools, poor roads, and inadequate support for high-tech operations.

This competitiveness factor points up another distinctive feature of American federalism. The other major federations (e.g., Canada, Australia, West Germany) provide special assistance to the poorer states to keep interstate tax and spending differentials from becoming too great. In the United States, however, we rely on interjurisdictional competition for economic development to perform this stabilizing role, simultaneously forcing high-tax states to slow down, while prompting low-spending states to accelerate on the public service side of the ledger, especially for education and physical infrastructure.

This federal hands-off policy with respect to interstate fiscal equalization will come under increasing criticism now that the poorer regions of the nation are no longer slowly closing the rich state–poor state gap, as they did between 1929 and 1979. In fact, since 1979, that gap has slowly widened because the wealthier states located in New England and the mid-Atlantic regions are once again growing at a faster rate than most states in other regions, especially the South. Without outside help, can the poorest states and localities be truly competitive? This issue poses another tough equity question for fend-for-yourself federalists.

No matter how the equity question is resolved, one thing appears fairly certain: the competition issue is not going to go away. In fact, competition for jobs and investment dollars is likely to become increasingly fierce because: (a) the U.S. economy is becoming more and more open to global competition, and (b) the recent and sharp cuts in federal income tax rates have substantially reduced the value of state and local tax deductions on the federal 1040. This development, in turn, is bound to increase the sensitivity of upper-income taxpayers and business firms to interstate and interlocal tax differentials.

The memory of the taxpayers' revolt and the squeeze on the federal budget also put a keener edge on interjurisdictional competition for jobs and economic development. In the post–Proposition 13 era, major tax hikes are still quite risky and the prospects for more aid from Washington are almost nil. Thus, the growth in the tax base generated by economic development stands out as a most attractive method for revenue enhancement. It should also be emphasized that bringing in new jobs and retaining existing jobs are becoming two of the most important tests of a successful state or local administration. In view of these political realities, it is highly unlikely that many governors or mayors would be willing to sign nonaggression pacts with their counterparts in neighboring jurisdictions.

Resiliency: Keeping the System Going

Now for the third distinctive feature of American federalism: the resiliency of state and local governments. In my judgment, the most underrated feature of our federal system is clearly the demonstrated ability of our fifty states and thousands of localities to absorb and then to rebound from regional and national shocks.

The fiscal resiliency of the fifty state systems can be easily documented. Since 1978, these state-local systems have absorbed the shock of the three Rs:

Revolt of the taxpayers—Proposition 13, etc.

Recession—the 1981–82 economic downturn, which was the sharpest since the Great Depression.

Reduction in federal aid flows.

More recently, many of the states have been hit hard by regional downturns. The farm states have been pinched severely by the agricultural recession and the energy states of the southwest have taken hard hits from the sharp drop in oil prices. Yet, despite all these shocks, the states as a collectivity are doing far better than most students of state and local finance would have predicted a few years ago.

The resiliency of our fifty state-local systems also comes through clearly when the fiscal fortunes of the federal government and the states are compared over time. If a modern Rip van Winkle had fallen into a deep sleep at the end of the Korean War and awakened recently, he would not believe the changes that have transformed our intergovernmental system.

Now, the state and localities are both playing the activist roles in education and welfare reform, and collecting well over one-half trillion dollars from their own resources. Even more surprising to the modern Rip van Winkle, however, would be the spectacle of the federal government mired down deeply in massive budget deficits because the Congress and the president cannot agree on a budget balancing strategy.

The remarkable state-local revenue raising performance since the end of World War II, summarized in Table 2.1, serves as the most persuasive example of resiliency. In 1946, the federal government dominated the intergovernmental tax field, collecting almost four times as much general revenue as all the states and local governments combined. By 1986, the state-local sector had almost drawn even with Washington's revenue raisers.

This steady state-local advance is especially noteworthy because it took place despite (a) the continued presence of a high level of federal revenue, (b) growing concern for interstate and interlocal competition, and (c) in recent years, the memory of the taxpayers' revolt.

Table 2.1

Reducing the Federal Revenue Lead:
Fifty-Year Governmental Trend, 1936–86
(revenues expressed as a percentage of GNP)

	Own-source general and trust fund revenue		Own-source general revenue		Federal aid to states and localities[b]
	Federal	State-local[a]	Federal	State-local[b]	
1936	6.2	10.2	6.1	8.9	1.2
1946	21.8	6.1	20.5	5.4	0.4
1956	18.9	8.9	17.1	7.3	0.8
1966	18.3	10.9	15.4	9.1	1.7
1976	18.7	14.4	13.8	11.6	3.2
1986	20.1	15.9	13.7	12.5	2.7

Source: GNP percentages are based on U.S. Bureau of the Census revenue reports.
[a]Excludes federal aid received by states and localities.
[b]Total state-local general revenue—own-source plus federal aid—now exceeds federal general revenue.

Looking Back

For one hundred forty years, the continued presence of a very small federal government provided conclusive evidence of the enduring effectiveness of constitutional constraints when strongly backed by the force of public opinion. As late as 1929, total federal spending amounted to 2.5 percent of GNP—about one-third the amount raised and spent that year by all the states and local governments.

Since 1929, American federalism has undergone the great transformation—the change from a small public sector with the federal government operating under tight constitutional wraps to a large public sector with the federal government legally free to enter into areas once considered either the private domain of the state-local sector or the exclusive preserve of the private sector. To put labels on this remarkable evolution, our intergovernmental system has moved over the last 60 years from Constitutional Federalism, through Crisis Federalism (1929–53), to Fiscal Federalism—an intergovernmental relationship in which Washington's influence over states and localities tends to expand and to contract with the rise and decline of federal aid flows.

As to be expected, the current state of federalism is not without its sharp critics. Those critics with a liberal point of view emphasize the equity imbalance: that fend-for-yourself federalism does poorly by those who are least able to fend for themselves—poor people and poor governments. Critics on the right (joined by many state and local officials) point to a menacing constitutional or power imbalance. They paint a grim scenario of things to come. A constitutionally unconstrained but financially strapped Congress is likely to be pushed by special interests to make ever increasing use of unfunded mandates and in this process transform elected state and local officials into Washington's hired hands. Why? Because now that the Supreme Court has flashed Congress the judicial green light, conservative federalists claim that states and localities have lost their last line of constitutional protection against the imposition of intrusive federal policies. Without the Court as the arbiter of state/congressional jurisdictional disputes, states and localities will now be forced to fight their own battles in the congressional arena—another example of fend-for-yourself federalism at work.

Neither these concerns about social inequities nor fears about future power grabs can obliterate a towering reality—the great transformation from small public sector/constitutional federalism to large public sector/fiscal federalism has not led us inexorably into the arms of a highly centralized national government, an Orwellian outcome many had predicted. On the contrary, fifty years after most of the constitutional and political constraints on Washington had collapsed, the resilient states and localities are very much alive and most of them are doing quite well. It is the national government that is experiencing a considerable degree of fiscal discomfort.

Why have state and local governments continued to fare so surprisingly well in the presence of a supposedly rapacious Washington long freed from its constitutional constraints? Why is Washington having such a difficult time strengthening its own general revenue system?

Five observations may at least partially answer these two questions.

> • *States and their localities never lost control of the "core" functions of domestic government.* As previously emphasized, they retained primary responsibility for the maintenance of law and order, the education of the youth, the regulation of domestic relations, the protection of public health, control of land use decisions, the promotion of state and local economic development policies, and the provision of regional and local public amenities (libraries, parks, museums).

• *On balance, the great tide of federal activism and federal aid dollars that swept across the state-local landscape during the golden era (1953–78) had a state-strengthening effect—not a state-weakening effect.* Southern states were liberated from the politics of racial segregation and all states benefited from the capacity-building effects of many of the new federal aid programs.

• *State government roots go down into the bedrock of the American federal system: the counties, the cities, the townships, the school districts, and the special districts.* State constitutional and statutory law and state financial aid flows stand out as powerful factors shaping local governmental policies. Much of the great diversity found in our federal system can be traced to the fact that each of our fifty state-local systems has its own set of unique characteristics.

• *Forced by frequent fiscal crises, states and localities have slowly but surely diversified and strengthened their revenue raising systems.* This strengthening of revenue systems is most evident at the state level. Most states now make fairly effective use of two primary sources of revenue: the individual income tax and the general sales tax. Own-source state and local revenue is the mother's milk of the American federal system.

• *Only a national crisis can provide the political cover federal policy makers apparently need before imposing a major general tax hike on the electorate; as the crisis recedes the tax raising advantage then shifts back to the state-local sector* (see Table 2.1). Over the last seventy years, Congress has gone to the individual income tax well for additional revenue only in the most dire situations: World War I, the Great Depression, World War II, the Korean War, and the Vietnam War. In striking contrast, state and local officials are constantly raising their taxes when confronted with state-wide and local crises.

Taken together, these five facts point to an upbeat conclusion: after two hundred years, the American federal system still possesses both great internal strengths and self-correcting characteristics. Why? While Washington's fiscal power is only infrequently strengthened (albeit massively) by a national crisis, states and local revenue systems are steadily strengthened (albeit modestly) by the relative frequency of state-wide and local fiscal crises.

3

Federalism and Urban Policy: The Intergovernmental Dialectic

RICHARD CHILD HILL

How has Urban America responded to a decade of the New Fiscal Federalism? The most striking changes in our intergovernmental system, I will argue, are connected to a shift in domestic government priorities from social welfare to economic growth. That shift in emphasis carries with it corresponding changes in (1) public aims; (2) political coalitions; (3) strategies for realizing public purposes; and (4) loci for initiating change within the intergovernmental system.

What accounts for the change in emphasis from social welfare to capital accumulation? The causes are to be found partly in the political arena, in the New Federalist attack on the welfare state. But the main cause is to be found in changes in the global economy and the international competitive position of the United States. Many labels have been used to characterize the nature of today's global economic transition: the Second Industrial Divide, post-Fordism, the Era of Human Capital, and so on; but they all connote the decline of U.S. hegemony in the world system in the face of competition from nations with comparable capacities to make productive use of technological advances, particularly in microelectronics. It is global economic change, more than anything else, that has pressured for a realignment of priorities in the U.S. federal system.

The New Federalism is a conservative strategy to combat the declining international position of the U.S. economy—reflected in shrinking productivity and profit rates, and expanding flows of capital abroad—through contraction and reorganization of the social welfare and social regulation policies advanced by popular movements in the 1960s and early 1970s, largely under the auspices of the Democratic party and largely targeted on central city populations. In the context of the global restructuring of capitalism, the Right has managed to appropriate "pro-

duction issues'': productivity, efficiency, competitiveness, and economic growth. The liberal opposition, on the other hand, has stressed
''equity issues'': social inequality and discrimination against minorities.
But in the face of the Right's continuing ability to set the national agenda
with policies to cut back welfare, marginalize national union power and
favor rising business sectors, liberals, too, have begun to promote a
development agenda.

The change in emphasis from a welfare to a developmental state is at
best a mixed blessing for Urban America. Associated with this shift in
public priorities and intergovernmental relations are patterns of growth
and decline, privilege and deprivation, power and dependency which do
not favor inner city populations and older industrial communities. My
purpose in this paper is to address the nature, causes and urban implications of the shift from a welfare oriented to a development oriented
federal system in the United States.

Federalism and Urban Policy

The history of city-state relations in western nations chronicles a recurring
conflict between central and local governments over the distribution of
political resources and authority. Through the course of time, a dialectic of
national expansion and local resistance has structured, undone, and restruc-
tured again complex, institutional patterns of cooperation, dependency, and
conflict among national, regional, and local governments.[1]

The history of U.S. federalism—the ''territorial allocation of government authority secured by constitutional guarantees''[2]—reveals a shifting mix of responsibilities and relationships among levels of
government.[3] Because officials at various levels of the U.S. federal
system share rather than divide up powers and functions, the intergovernmental distribution of resources and program responsibilities is a
persistent political issue. Changes in the structure of federalism are
invariably linked to changes in policies and programs. Indeed, political
attempts to change the distribution of responsibilities among governments usually reflect broader social conflicts over the substance of public
policy.[4]

Governmental autonomy is structured by constitutional, legal, and
administrative mechanisms. In the U.S. federal system, state governments, like the federal government, derive their authority directly from
the people. Therefore, as Elazar has argued,[5] states are substantially

immune from federal interference. Cities, on the other hand, are the constitutional creatures of the states. Because U.S. cities lack the autonomy afforded to federal and state governments, urban policies are strongly affected by alterations in the balance of policy initiative and programmatic activity between federal and state governments.

There is a contradiction built into the economic structure of federalism. Cities are less able to exert control over their internal economies than the federal government and must compete against one another for tax revenue. Intermunicipal competition for tax dollars ensures the predominance of business oriented growth policies at the local level. The national government, on the other hand, has a wider latitude for social policy formation.[6] Yet, in comparison to Washington officials, municipal leaders are closer to the people they serve and less able to neglect social hardship within their jurisdictions. This contradiction explains why national governments assume an expanded role in municipal life during periods of economic and social crisis. In fact, as Gurr and King cogently argued in *The State and the City*, the vitality of cities in advanced industrial democracies has increasingly been determined by the allocative decisions of national governments.

Federal responsibility for U.S. cities has expanded in two great waves during this century: the New Deal of the 1930s, and the Great Society of the 1960s.[7] Both were crisis periods when cities took on heightened political salience for the national government. The deeply depressed economy of the 1930s produced severe urban fiscal distress and threatened social disorder. In the 1960s, cities were rocked by collective action and racial strife over issues of civil rights and social empowerment. In both periods, public officials structured intergovernmental relations so as to foster direct relations between city residents and the federal government. Political alignments between mayors, big city congressional representatives and Washington bureaucrats funneled federal resources into urban areas afflicted by joblessness, poverty, blight, and crime.

During the New Deal and Great Society, Democratic national administrations overrode the interests and preferences of many state and local officials by articulating a national ideology of positive social intervention. Today, following the national ascendancy of two successive Republican administrations, the distribution of intergovernmental powers and resources is shaped by a different set of political objectives: to promote capital accumulation through greater reliance on market forces, deregulation and contraction in direct social spending.

From Great Society to New Federalism

Great Society programs were promulgated in an economic context characterized by stability and growth. The domestic economy was fueled by a system of mass production whose parameters were well known and assumed to be fixed and the United States reigned over the world economy. The social circumstance giving birth to Great Society programs, on the other hand, was urban conflict. A broad based civil rights movement was pressuring for minority access to institutions and empowerment within the urban political system.

According to a number of political analysts,[8] the political aim of the Great Society was to integrate Black voters into the Democratic party coalition through place targeted entitlement programs administered by Democratic urban regimes. The Great Society's public aims emphasized social welfare, equity, regulation, and the incorporation of disadvantaged and disenfranchised groups into the political process. These aims were to be achieved through a social services strategy. Social reform in health, housing, welfare, and other public sectors was to be carried forward by professionals claiming the technical expertise to solve urban problems. The core coalitions sustaining the Great Society were made up of social service professionals, managers of social service bureaucracies, congressional committees, and entitlement groups. Program initiatives came from the federal government whose outlays for a vast array of social programs were administered by state and local governments—the "foot soldiers" in the Great Society model of the welfare state.[9]

Even during the height of the Great Society, many state and local officials resisted, ignored, or reinterpreted federal attempts to impose nationally defined objectives[10] indicating a persistent conflict between local development interests and national redistributive aims.[11] And escalating cost of financing the Vietnam War further weakened public support for Great Society domestic initiatives. Republican victories in the early 1970s ushered in a national administration bent on dissolving Democratic party alliances between national officialdom and local urban and ethnic groups. In 1972, Republican President Richard Nixon attacked "national purpose" legislation and called for a "New Federalism." Nixon's New Federalism would replace categorical programs that specified federal purposes in granting assistance to localities with general revenue sharing and block grants that increased the discretion of local officials in utilizing federal funds. While the Nixon administration cloaked the New Federalism in appealing "local control" rhetoric, the change from categorical to block grants was really designed to break the connection between program and place and thereby undercut the Democratic party's urban coalition.

Upon entering the White House in the late 1970s, Democrat Jimmy Carter attempted to rejuvenate the party's urban coalition with policies targeted to declining industrial regions of traditional Democratic strength.[12] An excess unemployment factor was added to the revenue-sharing formula to benefit economically distressed cities. Comprehensive Employment Training Assistance and Community Development Block Grant programs were expanded. An Urban Development Action Grant program was initiated to stimulate private investment in declining cities. But Carter's urban efforts fell victim to a global economic slump and a domestic tax revolt. With the introduction of a "New Partnership" policy in 1978, the Carter administration shifted focus from revitalizing cities to revitalizing business and industry.

Reagan's New Federalism

When Ronald Reagan assumed office at the beginning of the 1980s, he resurrected Richard Nixon's New Federalism and intensified the conservative attack upon the programs and institutions of the Great Society. Reagan's New Federalists attacked the Great Society on a number of fronts. First, they mounted a major ideological assault on the liberal values of the Great Society, particularly the public commitment to equality of opportunity and the political empowerment of marginalized groups.

As Andrew Kopkind[13] has argued, the Reagan administration assailed virtually all the liberal institutions that had helped define and shape American culture since the New Deal, "the press, the churches, unions, academia, local public education, urban government, philanthropic foundations, the artistic establishment, Hollywood, publishing, federal service, the liberal professions and their organizations." Even the term, "liberalism," was ridiculed and held to be incompatible with polite political discourse. Government, Reagan policy analysts claimed, was too large, too expensive, and too intrusive. They contrasted the public realm unfavorably with private and localistic institutions: business, family, church, and voluntary associations.[14] Private institutions conveyed the Reagan administration's value preferences: "competitive enterprise over collective endeavor, the family unit over the heterogeneous community, male authority over sexual democracy, patriotism over internationalism, selfishness over altruism, having over sharing.''[15]

Second, New Federalists attacked the Great Society's "services strategy" for ameliorating urban problems. According to the Reaganites, the services strategy drained public resources, sponsored dependency upon the government and undermined traditional social values, particularly localism.

In place of the services strategy, Reagan's urban policy architects substituted public choice theory—a market model of government whereby cities are likened to business firms and voting expresses individual tastes for government products. Competition among local governments and between municipalities and private firms produce efficiency and effectiveness in service provision, according to public choice advocates. In their view, the increasing size and power of government was responsible for America's falling productivity and rising inflation during the 1970s. Reducing the size of government and expanding the scope of the private market would lead to increased government efficiency, increased productivity throughout the economy, and increased international competitive power for the U.S. economy.[16]

Third, the New Federalists attacked the group promoting the services strategy—the service professionals, whom Reaganites dubbed a "new class" of "social engineers" and they attacked the federal-city coalition that sustained the Great Society. Government grew, according to Reagan policy analysts like E.S. Savas, because of the self-interest and power of service providers, clients, politicans, bureaucrats, and the liberal intellectual elite. Government monopolies in the post office, police, public housing, and elsewhere spent more than was required to get the work done and were inherently inefficient. [17]

Reagan and the Republican right wing viewed Great Society programs as government sponsored social engineering that undermined traditional values and social relationships. The Reaganites contrasted federal bureaucrats, social planners and urban clientele groups unfavorably with Main Street institutions: small towns, small businesses and local voluntary associations. For New Federalists, Great Society social programs added up to "political nestbuilding."

Because federal grant programs were implemented through a "cooperative federalism," the intergovernmental system became a major target for the new Federalists. Through program cuts, the New Federalists engaged in a conscious effort to "defund the left"—to bankrupt the social action, civil rights movement, and coalitions of public service clients and providers depending upon federal funds. The Reaganites also sought to "disrupt the left" through block grants forcing interest groups out of the Capitol to state and local levels which were unfamiliar and more conservative terrain.[18] Decentralization, the new Federalists expected, would hold down state and local spending through interstate competition for investment and through closer proximity to taxpayers.

In the view of Andrew Kopkind, Reagan's constituency consisted of people who felt "their power diminished, their profits dissipated, their mobility curtailed, and their security endangered" during the Great Society and Vietnam Era. Included here, Kopkind argues, are whites and men in general, conservative politicians in both parties, the military and defense establishment; some Jews, most European ethnics, and young executives. At the cornerstone of Reagan's institutional base stood fundamentalist churches and their rapidly growing school system, right wing foundations, think tanks, broadcasting and publishing outlets, volunteer and charitable institutions, and an ideologically oriented, nouveau business elite rooted in the south and western regions.[19]

For critics of Reaganism with a class perspective, the New Federalism boiled down to a "new class war."[20] Deregulating and contracting the welfare state was a strategy to raise profits by reconnecting the relationship between unemployment and wages—a relationship broken to some extent by welfare state programs. Through decentralizing government authority, New Federalists hoped to drag program levels and eligibility criteria down to the lowest state level by forcing states and localities to compete for capital while the federal government escaped the onus of direct cuts in programs. And by breaking the connection between economic and political rights, privatization and decentralization were designed to contract and depoliticize the state as an arena of class conflict.

The Decline of Social Welfare

The New Federalists mounted a three pronged assault on the Great Society. They set out to (1) deeply cut social programs; (2) undercut indirect federal support for organizations that represented Great Society clientele groups; and (3) devolve the policy-making terrain to the states by folding categorical grants into block grants. What have the New

Federalists managed to accomplish over the past decade?

Timothy Conlan's recent study[21] indicates that overall domestic spending continued to increase during the Reagan administration but the rate of growth diminished. Behind the growth, however, were changes in domestic spending priorities. The New Federalists increased spending on some programs and deeply cut on others. Grants-in-aid were hit the hardest. Within grants, payments to governments for the provision of services received the largest cuts. Federal grants to state and local governments fell 30 percent between 1980 and 1987.

Reagan's expenditure cuts, it should be noted, accelerated trends already begun in the last Carter years. Federal grants to state and local governments peaked in fiscal 1978, Carter's second year. As a percent of the federal budget, they fell from 17.0 percent in 1978 to 10.8 percent in 1987; as a percent of GNP the drop was from 3.5 percent in 1978 to 2.5 percent in 1987. The largest cuts were concentrated in community and economic development, education, social services, employment and training. Between 1980 and 1985, outlays for community and regional development fell 40 percent and expenditures on education, employment and training, and social services fell by one-third.[22]

New Federalist program cuts targeted the ''foot soldiers of the Great Society's service strategy''[23]—the northern industrial states and big cities with large education and social service bureaucracies. Particularly hard hit were the Great Society's hallmark urban programs. Community services, the descendant of the Community Action Program, was cut by 50 percent. Local public works and regional development grants were practically eliminated. Urban renewal, training and employment services were cut by two-thirds. Within education, bilingual and compensatory education took the biggest cuts.

The Reagan administration also tried to undercut subsidies for federally oriented organizations that mobilized the poor, like the Legal Services Corporation. Block grants were used to push interest groups out of Washington onto a less familiar policy-making terrain. The aim was to reduce the overall magnitude of public sector activity by forcing ''political decisions and the struggles accompanying them down to the state and local government level.''[24] New Federalist cuts in state-local aid were targeted at municipalities not state governments. Abandoned by Washington, many city officials turned to their states for support. Not all state governments tried to compensate for the drop in urban federal revenues but some did. In 1988, fifteen states adopted spending or tax proposals to help local governments, including assistance for health, welfare, and the courts. Total state aid to cities, not counting welfare and education outlays, rose from $8 to $15 billion between 1978 and 1986. Even so, federal cutbacks in domestic spending considerably outdistanced total state aid to cities during the 1980s.[25]

While the New Federalists managed to contract the federal-city policy network and heighten the misery of the urban poor, they have thus far failed to dislodge the basic New Deal/Great Society safety net spanning social insurance, public welfare, environmental protection and individual rights. On the other hand, by forcing local governments to become far more dependent on their own revenues and state aid, the Reagan administration exacerbated fiscal inequalities among governments within the federal system.[26] Between 1981 and 1986, city revenues increased from $287 to $434 billion with state contributions to city revenues rising from $90 to $126.8 billion—much of it for education and welfare.[27]

States with growing economies have been able to help local governments more than economically troubled states. Louisiana, afflicted by the global slump in the oil industry, illustrates the fiscal difficulties facing economically troubled states and cities. Between 1986 and 1988, Louisiana cities lost $150 million in federal aid and $50 million in state aid with additional cuts made at a special legislative session. New Orleans' budget has fallen by $40 million since 1985 and the city has cut 600 employees as a result. Nonetheless, New Orleans continues to face a $19 million deficit and with a sales tax already at 9 percent the city finds it difficult to raise additional tax revenue.

But even growth states, like New Jersey, aren't adequately helping their poorer cities, like Camden and Newark. New Jersey's older cities are trapped in a cycle of high property taxes and low services. But since the six largest New Jersey cities have only 13 percent of the state's population, revising the state property tax system to help solve big city problems is next to impossible in the face of suburban opposition.[28]

The Rise of Fiscal Welfare

If all the New Federalists had managed to do was impose deep cuts in Great Society urban programs, they wouldn't have altered the federal-city policy relationship very much. So long as allocation by congressional appropriation and implementation through the usual agencies continued, budget cuts would simply have resulted in increased competition among groups representing urban interests and heightened group efforts to establish close clientele relations with the congressional committees and bureaucratic agencies that control the funds—a continuation, albeit at a considerably reduced level of resources, of the Great Society urban policy network.

That is not the whole story, however. Apart from eliminating some urban programs and reducing others, New Federalists have distinguished themselves from Great Society activists by the extent to which they have allocated public resources through tax rather than direct budget expenditures and by their reliance on the market rather than planned public interventions.[29] According to Michael Smith,[30] tax expenditures now constitute the equivalent of one-third of U.S. federal budget expenditures, up from one-fourth in the mid-1970s. In Smith's view, "fiscal welfare—the allocation of tax benefits to private individuals, groups, or organizations in order to get them to pursue a public purpose" displaced social welfare as the principal urban policy tool under the Reagan administration.

As Susan Clarke has argued,[31] "on-budget" expenditures that are authorized, appropriated, and reviewed periodically by Congress contrast sharply with "off-budget" initiatives—the tax credits and credit programs established by the federal government. Once authorized, off-budget allocations are automatic, seemingly costless benefits granted to certain groups without periodic appropriations. They entail revenue losses for the federal government and costs associated with defaults on federal direct and guaranteed loans.

The New Federalists increasingly used off-budget expenditures in key urban policy areas, including education, training, employment, social services, and neighborhood development. Of the reduced funds New Federalists made available to cities, Clarke[32] notes that more and more were allocated through processes that were neither accessible nor accountable to urban interest groups. Politically, the effect was to remove budgetary processes from political pressures and channel the activities of local organizations to areas favored by tax credits and credit guarantees. Socially, the effect was to redistribute government benefits from public service providers and the urban poor to sectoral growth alliances among developers, entrepreneurs, bankers, and trade unions.[33]

Urban neighborhood policy illustrates the shift from social to fiscal welfare.[34] Neighborhood revitalization has been a key element of national urban policy since the New Deal. The Great Society policy makers viewed neighborhoods as social, political and economic entities, as well as administrative vehicles for the nation's urban programs. Social needs and citizen participation had a high priority in Great Society efforts to revitalize declining urban neighborhoods. The Community Action Program, established in 1964, bypassed local officials to directly fund Community Action Agencies and required representation of poor people on the planning boards.

During the Carter administration, the local community was viewed as a "third sector" partner with business and government in revitalization efforts. Government's role was to increase neighborhood self-help capacities so as to strengthen their role in implementing national urban policy.

Reagan's New Federalists viewed neighborhoods not as spatial, political, social, or administrative units but as "congested loci of economic exchange."[35] Economic growth was the solution to problems in cities. Since government involvement hampered the efficient use of local resources, government programs should be withdrawn and local entrepreneurs encouraged to step in and take their place.[36]

The New Federalists reduced federal support for urban neighborhoods by eliminating HUD's office of Neighborhoods, Voluntary Associations and Consumer Protection, by eliminating the HUD assistant secretary position responsible for neighborhood policy under Carter, and by closing the Office of Neighborhood Development. But even as they cut direct outlays on neighborhoods, Reaganites increased off-budget neighborhood expenditures. The enterprise zone strategy, a congeries of tax incentives and regulation waivers to attract private investment to deteriorated urban areas, is an example of the spatially targeted off-budget strategy. It is also an example of Reagan's market oriented policy approach. As Clarke has noted, whether new tax revenues from new business activity stimulated by an enterprise zone program can offset loss of revenue through tax expenditures depends not upon the program design and implementation but upon the effectiveness of the tax incentives and the vitality of the local market.

Pursuing neighborhood revitalization through fiscal welfare was a conscious Reagan strategy to diminish political activity in urban neighborhoods. Direct spending programs required at least nominal citizen participation; tax measures did not. The technical complexities of the tax code changed neighborhood politics from a struggle over distribution of direct subsidies to a more limited debate over whether the targeted tax benefits should be granted and to whom. Neighborhood organizers found it difficult to mobilize groups around these "invisible benefits" and little information was available on them.[37]

By using the tax code rather than direct expenditures and by emphasizing market strategies rather than planned intervention, the New Federalists did not eliminate neighborhood involvement in urban revitalization efforts. Rather, the Reagan administration organized a different type of federal-city relationship. Tax tools and market implementation strategies forced neighborhood groups out of the political arena into the marketplace. With declining federal funds, public officials had fewer dollars to distribute. Political organization and influence became less significant for neighborhood groups. To become successful in the marketplace, neighborhood groups must adopt profit oriented management styles, including more centralized decision making and shorter time horizons. In sum, neighborhood organizations become market intermediaries rather than political representives of local interests.

The Developmental State

While Reagan's New Federalism was a deeply ideological attack on the liberal institutions of the Great Society, it was actually an economic wind that filled Reagan's political sails. The American economy slumped from one crisis to another during the 1970s and Reagan was elected in the midst of the worst economic downturn since the Great Depression. Global overcapacity and increasing international competition brought on a crisis of profitability for U.S. businesses. Reagan's supporters claimed there was too little capital available for modernization and held the welfare state responsible for absorbing scarce resources and sapping worker productivity. A return to the market was the proffered solution.

The New Federalism will endure only to the extent that New Federalists can facilitate the reordering of U.S. economic and political institutions to match the challenges of a new global economy. On that fundamental issue, conservative Republicans are under challenge from another political direction, "neo-Progressivism," an outlook recently scrutinized in some detail by David Osborne.[38] In contrast to the New Federalists, neo-Progressives argue that cities, states, and regions that emphasize low taxes, low labor costs, and stringent fiscal policies are out-of-touch with the demands of a new international economy characterized by a microelectronic revolution and a transition from mass to flexible system production.[39] The world's poorer countries cannot be outcompeted on wages or taxes. Rather, to be internationally competitive, the U.S. must possess a technologically advanced, high value added economy that requires a strong tax system, hefty investments in education, and social expenditures on research and reliable physical plant. State policy making, neo-Progressives argue, must therefore be central, not incidental, to economic development in the United States.[40]

Neo-Progressivism, Osborne[41] argues, is a new political synthesis born of a dialectic between Welfare State liberalism and New Federalist conservatism. Over the past two decades "activist liberals have gradually moved from a focus on poor, urban communities to a broader concern for economic growth." The 1960s were a time of struggle for participation and empowerment within social programs—unemployment insurance, welfare, health care—while the industrial system was characterized by stability. The 1980s are a time of economic transformation. The world economy is governed not by the hegemonic power of the United States but by fierce rivalry among nations. What is most needed now are programs to lead business and labor to embrace change.

Neo-Progressives look to national competitors in Western Europe, and particularly to Japan, for government role models.[42] Chalmers Johnson[43] has aptly described Japan as a "developmental state." In contrast to a U.S.-style "regulatory state" which emphasizes rules and procedures, the developmental state sets sight on substantive economic goals and takes a strategic approach to the economy. Industrial policy, the promotion of industrial structures that will enhance a nation's international competitive power, takes priority.

Among the essential features of Japan's developmental state is an elite bureaucracy, trained in the best schools of policy and management and educated in law and economics. Japan's elite bureaucrats rotate among jobs frequently and retire early. Their duties are to identify industries to be developed, identify the best means for developing them and supervise competition in strategic sectors. In Japan, Johnson argues, politicians reign and bureaucrats rule. Politicians absorb interest-group demands, allowing bureaucrats to plan more flexibly.

Japan's developmental state is characterized by a cooperative relationship between government and business. Ownership and management is left in private hands, thereby maintaining competition, while the state sets goals and shapes market behavior through incentives. Japan's market conforming methods of state intervention include (1) selective access to government financing; (2) targeted tax breaks; (3) government supervised investment coordination to keep all participants profitable; (4) government's equitable allocation of burdens during adversity; (5) government assistance in the commercialization of products; and (6) government assistance when industry begins to decline.[44]

In accord with Japan's developmental state, the public aims of U.S. neo-Progressives revolve around a "rekindling of economic development." Economic growth, productivity, and innovation are neo-Progressive watchwords. In Osborne's summary, neo-Progressives emphasize: (1) growth with equity; (2) market solutions; (3) nonbureaucratic methods for implementing programs; (4) fiscal moderation; (5) investment rather than spending; (6) expansion of opportunity rather than redistribution of outcomes; (7) social adjustment rather than a safety net.

In contrast to the Great Society's social program emphasis, neo-Progressives seek to achieve public aims through business and workplace strategies. State activities and incentives are designed to shape market behavior in conformance with public policy. Public incentives run the gamut from simple tax breaks for publicly desired investment behavior, to an array of state provided business assistance services, to fairly sophisticated sectoral planning.[45] Leading state actors are economic development professionals lodged in government, private, and third sector organizations. Departments of commerce rather than social services hold the public trump card. Tripartite coalitions among business, labor, and government representatives sustain the neo-Progressive strategy.

The neo-Progressive outlook is presently strongest among state government officials. Osborne sees an analogue to current political events in the Progressive Era at the turn of the century. Then, the states intervened at the local level and offered programmatic models that were eventually adopted by the federal government. Neo-Progressives speak of a new partnership among federal, state, and local governments. The federal government engages in macroeconomic policy management—fiscal, monetary, tax, and trade—while state and local governments engage in microeconomic intervention.[46]

Neo-Progressives defend their version of federalism on the grounds that it corresponds to the actual structure of the U.S. economy. The United States is a tapestry of regional economies, each radiating out from a city or network of cities.[47] Each regional economy possesses a unique mix of industries, labor markets, educational institutions, and capital markets. The design of government programs should therefore be specific to a region. National "cookie cutter" models won't work. State government is closest to the regional level but there are limits to what states and localities can do because interstate competition contrains their tax base. The federal government should enter to buttress state efforts and deal with issues that are national in scope.

The rise of activist local developmental states is partly a consequence of the New Federalism. That is ironic since the Reagan administration liked "little Leviathans" no better than big ones. While the nation stumbled from one economic crisis to another during the 1970s and early 1980s, Washington continued to disdain arguments favoring industrial policies. Since the federal government covers a broad and diverse economic terrain, national policy makers could aggregate out economic decline in one part of the nation by statistically combining it with economic growth elsewhere. Officials in states afflicted by the economic crisis didn't have that option; they had to act.

State officials had the capacity to respond if they were so inclined. As Neal Pierce has noted,[48] "constitutionally there isn't much that a state can't regulate, finance, foster or discourage if it chooses to do so." And federal actions in recent years had enhanced the powers of the states significantly. Congress had given state officials central roles as planners, administrators, and implementors for major federal domestic programs and intergovernmental regulatory policies.

The New Federalists thought federal cutbacks, interstate competition, and local control would restrain government action. Many states reacted instead by plunging into uncharted industrial policy waters and aggressively addressing issues of economic development and educational reform. In science and technology, several states, including Pennsylvania, Ohio, Massachussets, Indiana, New Jersey, Michigan, and North Carolina upgraded their research and development capacity through targeted university centers of excellence, research parks in microelectronics and biotechnologies, science-based business development centers, new venture capital funds, and use of state pension funds for small business development.[49] And between 1982 and 1986, state governments financed school reform efforts to the tune of $12 billion.[50]

Many states are moving away from smokestack chasing toward sophisticated conceptions of what is involved in economic development and making themselves more accountable for the health of their regional economies. In the view of one experienced observer of state and local government,[51] this represents an "historic shift" from states and cities as service providers to states and cities as economic development innovators, from state intervention in social reproduction to state intervention in economic production.

Future Urban Prospects

The huge deficits run up by the Reagan administration make it likely that today's federal retrenchment will endure well into the twenty-first century, according to many policy analysts.[52] In Pierce's view,[53] an era of federal retrenchment and deficit politics ensures that neo-Progressives will continue to operate chiefly at the state and local level, as during the 1920s when states were hailed as "laboratories of democracy" for their experimentation with progressive programs. Should this forecast prove accurate, neo-Progressive state administrations are the cities' best hope for the foreseeable future.

The prospects for troubled cities in neo-Progressive run states don't seem all that bright. For one thing, neo-Progressive politicians haven't been very successful in forging state-city urban policy networks. Neo-Progressives acknowledge that jobs must be created in depressed urban areas, dislocated workers retrained, and welfare recipients employed. And they point approvingly to Roosevelt, who did this by bringing middle class Progressives and working class Democratic machines together. But because neo-Progressives come from white, educated, professional backgrounds and evince a cerebral and technocratic political style, they are separated by class and culture from industrial workers and minorities.[54]

Moreover, the economic change neo-Progressives advocate threatens industrial workers and is irrelevant to the poor. Neo-Progressives reject the anti–big-business populism that helped tie past urban coalitions together. Today's popular consensus, they argue, is that big business has been wounded by foreign competition and is in need of help. Therefore, the best means to forge a new urban coalition is to reshape the marketplace to serve the needs of workers and minorities while "embracing economic growth and fiscal moderation."

A second critical issue is whether "growth with equity" is really possible under developmental state parameters, as neo-Progressives suggest, or whether we are more likely to see an intensification in the

United States of the inequality that characterizes the two sides of the corporate divide in Japan.[55] Neo-Progressives are as committed to tax expenditure policy tools as the New Federalists. Their chief concern is that government subsidies to business have not been sufficiently coordinated or linked to the performance of the enterprise.[56]

Robert Reich, a policy theorist held in considerable esteem by neo-Progressives, has noted that ''inkind company benefits—government tax expenditures—now include health insurance, pension plans, group life insurance, subsidized cafeteria food, recreation facilities, home mortgage subsidies, relocation assistance, group legal services, children's private schooling, child care facilities, assistance to spouses of transferred employees to find new jobs, psychiatric counseling, and industry social workers dealing with alcohol, family and drug problems.'' A rising percentage of employee compensation comes from this government backed, company administered social wage; in 1966 it amounted to 17 percent, in 1982 it came to 28 percent; and today it is as high as 40 percent in some large corporations.

Reich argues that the ''work community is replacing the geographic community'' as the central channel for government policy, and he favors that trajectory. Yet Reich also notes that unemployed and low income people are left out of the fiscal welfare system because they don't work for major companies. In 1987, U.S. income inequality, as measured by the ratio of the top 10 percent to the bottom 40 percent income share, was at its highest level since income data collection began in 1947.[57] If inequalities in the social wage, linked to the substitution of fiscal welfare for social welfare, were made apparent, real income inequality would be seen to be much higher still.

A third consideration is that neo-Progressive development policies are underwriting new patterns of uneven growth and decline in the nation's metropolitan areas. State officials are attempting to promote high technology industries to restructure their regional economies by investing in ''Science Cities'' or ''Technopolises.'' Apart from heavy government infrastructure and research subsidies, technopolises have in common strong business/university ties, large concentrations of scientific and engineering talent, and lush, greenfield locations on the periphery of large urban areas.[58] Because high technology industries are not locating in the same places where traditional manufacturing industries are declining, state supported restructuring is fostering new patterns of uneven urban development.

Michigan, a state administered by a prototypical neo-Progressive governor, is a case in point.[59] In Michigan, hi-tech entrepreneurs and state development offficals are promoting a metro-Detroit suburban corridor as a "Silicon Valley in Southeast Michigan for durable goods equipment suppliers."[60] Dubbed "Automation Alley" by state officials, the corridor already hosts the largest concentration of machine vision and robotics firms in the United States. According to a recent study by the state's Industrial Technology Institute, 76 percent of Michigan's high-tech automation companies are located in just four Detroit area counties; the vast majority of those cluster in Automation Alley; and only 6 percent are located inside the central city of Detroit.

Oakland Technology Park anchors the northwest pole of Automation Alley. Linked to Oakland University, spanning 1,800 acres and housing $2 billion in research and development facilities for robotics, engineering, automation, and advanced manufacturing applications, Oakland Technology Park numbers among the largest and fastest growing research and development sites in the United States. The park will generate an estimated 52,000 jobs by the mid-1990s.

This state subsidized high-tech economic restructuring is reinforcing the flow of capital away from Detroit's central city and into the northwest Oakland County suburbs. In 1960, the city of Detroit held 50 percent of the region's assessed valuation, Oakland County's share was 14 percent. By 1980, the city of Detroit's share had plummeted to 18 percent while Oakland County's had grown to 38 percent.[62]

The city of Detroit has recently put forward a "Strategic Plan" focused upon six problem areas: race, crime, education, jobs and development, housing, and image.[63] Based upon a municipal-business partnership, the plan fails to frame the city's problems in regional terms. Yet Detroit is now imbedded in a polycentric regional economy whose growth poles are outside the central city. The city of Detroit is unlikely to move forward with its development plan in the absence of a regional investment effort with strong state involvement, including legislation which links state tax subsidies for suburban economic growth to matching funds for central city revitalization.[64]

Neo-Progressives say growth policies must come first and lay the institutional foundations for the new economic era. Incorporation of those left out will come later. This sounds like a technocratic version of the old, discredited "trickle-down" theory; or, as Michael Harrington once called it, the politics of "malign neglect."[65]

Notes

1. Ted Robert Gurr and Desmond King, *The State and the City* (London: Macmillan, 1987).

2. Samuel Beer, "Introduction," in Timothy Conlan, *New Federalism: Intergovernmental Reform from Nixon to Reagan* (Washington, DC: The Brookings Institution, 1988).

3. Fiscal federalism refers to the territorial distribution and performance of the economic functions of government, including stabilization, allocation, and redistribution. See Wallace A. Oates, *Fiscal Federalism* (New York: Harcourt, Brace, Jovanovich, 1972).

4. Timothy Conlan, *New Federalism: Intergovernmental Reform from Nixon to Reagan* (Washington, DC: The Brookings Institution, 1988), chapter 1.

5. Daniel Elazar, *American Federalism: A View from the States* (New York: Harper & Row, 1984).

6. Paul E. Peterson, *City Limits* (Chicago: University of Chicago Press, 1981).

7. John Mollenkopf, *The Contested City* (Princeton: Princeton University Press, 1983).

8. Frances Piven and Richard Cloward, *Regulating the Poor* (New York: Vintage, 1971); Frances Piven and Richard Cloward, *The New Class War* (New York: Pantheon, 1982); and Michael Peter Smith, *City, State and Market* (Oxford: Basil-Blackwell, 1988).

9. Beer, "Introduction," p. xvii.

10. Peterson, *City Limits*.

11. For example, should city land be used for federal low income housing or for local development projects?

12. Smith, *City, State and Market*, pp. 99–102.

13. Andrew Kopkind, "The Age of Reaganism" *The Nation* 14 (September 1988).

14. E.S. Savas, *Privatization: The Key to Better Government* (Chatham, NJ: Chatham House Publishers, 1987), p. 26.

15. Kopkind, "The Age of Reaganism."

16. E.S. Savas was the principal author of Reagan's national urban policy. Formerly a political scientist at Columbia University, Savas worked on community development efforts in New York City before becoming the under secretary at Housing and Urban Development in the Reagan administration. Savas presents his policy views in *Privatization: The Key to Better Government*. Savas's role in the Reagan administration is presented in Roger S. Ahlbrandt, "Ideology and the Reagan Administration's First National Urban Policy Report," *Journal of the American Planning Association* 50, 4 (Autumn 1984), 479–84.

17. Savas, *Privatization*, chapter 2.

18. Conlan, *New Federalism*, pp. 223–24.

19. Kopkind, "The Age of Reaganism."

20. Piven and Cloward, *The New Class War*.

21. Conlan, *New Federalism*, pp. 153–54.

22. Ibid., p. 157.

23. Beer, "Introduction," p. xviii.

24. Conlan, *New Federalism*, p. 158.

25. Federal cutbacks during the 1980s totaled $30 billion for general revenue sharing, UDAG grants, and Community Development Block grants, alone. See John W. Moore, "Crazy-Quilt Federalism," *National Journal* (November 26, 1988), p. 3001.

26. Thomas R. Swartz, "A New Urban Crisis in the Making," *Challenge* (September/October 1987), 34–41.

27. Moore, "Crazy-Quilt Federalism," p. 3003.

28. Ibid., p. 3004.

29. Susan E. Clarke, "Neighborhood Policy Options: The Reagan Agenda," *Journal of the American Planning Association* (Autumn 1984), 493–501.

30. Smith, *City, State and Market*, p. 31.

31. Clarke, "Neighborhood Policy Options," p. 31.

32. Ibid.

33. Smith, *City, State and Market*, pp. 49–50. Smith further argues that the shift from direct social policy to fiscal policies to induce private business to achieve public policy goals entails a transfer of the public tax burden from corporations to individual workers. This seems doubtful since corporations, at least those in oligopolistic sectors of the economy, pass on taxes to workers (as consumers) through price increases in any case. Workers, particularly those outside the organized sectors of the economy, are disadvantaged either way.

34. Housing policy provides another case illustration. See Elizabeth A. Roistacher, "A Tale of Two Conservatives: Housing Policy Under Reagan and Thatcher," *Journal of the American Planning Association* (Autumn 1984), 485–492. For example, four times more subsidies are indirectly transferred to home owners through the tax code than to renters through direct government housing policies. See Smith, *City, State and Market*, p. 42.

35. Clarke, "Neighborhood Policy Options," p. 495.

36. Stuart M. Butler, "Neighborhood Groups and the Enterprise Zone," *Policy Dispatch* 2 (September 1981), 1–2.

37. For example, as Clarke has observed, the Internal Revenue Service does not collect information on the spatial impact of tax expenditures.

38. David Osborne, *Laboratories of Democracy* (Boston: Harvard Business School Press, 1988).

39. Neo-Progressive thinking on these matters has been heavily influenced by the "Harvard-MIT axis." In particular, see Robert Reich, *The New American Frontier* (New York: Times Books, 1983); and Michael Piore and Charles Sabel, *The Second Industrial Divide* (New York: Basic Books, 1984).

40. For example, see Neil R. Pierce, "The States: Are They Fulfilling Their Economic Development Potential?" *Economic Development Commentary* (Summer 1986), pp. 3–6.

41. Osborne, *Laboratories of Democracy*, p. 32.

42. In a number of European countries, the national state intervenes to promote urban and regional development through economic planning, infrastructure incentives, subsidies, relocation grants, investment allowances and direct state investment and management of enterprises. For a discussion on this point, see Gurr and King, *The State and the City*, chapter 1.

43. Chalmers Johnson, *MITI and the Japanese Miracle: The Growth of Industrial Policy, 1925–1975* (Stanford: Stanford University Press, 1982).

44. Ibid., pp. 312–14.

45. For example, see Beth Siegel, Andrew Reamer, and Mona Hochberg, "Sectoral Strategies: Targeting Key Industries," *Economic Development Commentary* (Winter 1987), 8–13.

46. Osborne, *Laboratories of Democracy*, p. 326.

47. For a defense of this viewpoint that neo-Progressives find appealing, see Jane Jacobs, *Cities and the Wealth of Nations* (New York: Random House, 1984).

48. Pierce, "The States," pp. 3–6.

49. Osborne, *Laboratories of Democracy*, part 1, pp. 21–248.

50. Pierce, "The States," p. 5.

51. Ibid., p. 6.

52. Lawrence J. Haas, "Putting It Off," *National Journal*, November 19, 1988, pp. 2928–2932; D.J. Jacobetti, "The Federal Budget Deficit: Impacts of the Reagan Era Budgets on the State of Michigan," House Appropriations Committee, Michigan House of Representatives, Lansing, Michigan (August 15, 1988), pp. 3379–87; and David Rapp, "Is Anyone Really Trying to Balance the Budget?" *Congressional Quarterly* 46, 48 (November 26, 1988).

53. Pierce, "The States," p. 6.

54. Osborne characterizes neo-Progressives as socially liberal, economically pragmatic, skeptical of big government, big labor, big business, supportive of entrepreneurship, change oriented, environmentalist, and individualistic.

55. For a discussion of dualism in Toyota Motor Corporation's production system in Japan, see Kuniko Fujita and Richard Child Hill, "Global Production and Regional 'Hollowing Out,' in Japan," *Comparative Urban & Community Research* 2 (1989), pp. 200–230.

56. Reich, *The New American Frontier,* chapter 2.

57. "Comparing Inequality," *Dollars & Sense*, January–February 1989, p. 23.

58. Manuel Castells, ed., *High Technology, Space and Society* (Beverly Hills: Sage Publications, 1985); and Kuniko Fujita, "The Technopolis: High Technology and Regional Development in Japan," *International Journal of Urban and Regional Research* 2, 4 (December 1988), 566–94.

59. Osborne, *Laboratories of Democracy,* chapter 5.

60. Ibid., p. 162.

61. Sean McAlinden, Dan Luria, and Mark Everett, "Michigan's Automation Supply Sector: A Resource for Automobile Supplier," *Auto-in-Michigan Newsletter* 3, 1 (January 1988): 1–8.

62. Joe Darden, Richard Child Hill, June Thomas, and Richard Thomas, *Detroit: Race and Uneven Development* (Philadelphia: Temple University Press, 1987), chapter 2.

63. City of Detroit, *Report of the Detroit Strategic Planning Project* (Detroit: n.p., 1987).

64. Linkage—exacting concessions from developers for city social needs in return for permitting them to build on choice parcels of land—has spread rapidly around the nation. Officials managing high growth cities have been able to get downtown developers to contribute to low income housing, job training, placement for minorities, and child care facilities in return for zoning clearances or permits. A state plan linking suburban growth to central city revitalization is similarly needed.

65. Michael Harrington, *The Other America* (Baltimore: Penguin, 1962).

———— 4 ————

Changing Federalism:
Trends and Interstate Variations

ROY W. BAHL, JR.

Every administration brings a new federalism with it. Most of the fanfare surrounds the announced programs that redefine the public financing roles of the federal, state, and local governments. The Johnson administration promoted poverty programs and Nixon's adopted General Revenue Sharing. Carter's bypassed the state governments in creating the big, direct, urban aid programs—CETA, ARFA, and local public works—and later began the retrenchment in federal aid to state and local governments and grant consolidation. The Reagan administration made bigger inroads into grant consolidation, continued the grant retrenchment, cut away at the deductibility subsidy to state and local governments, and shifted the balance of fiscal power back to the state level by abolishing direct local aid and the remnants of general revenue sharing.

Such announced changes, however, are only part of the story of what brings about changes in American intergovernmental structure, and possibly not even the most important part. Federal macroeconomic policies, designed to influence other aspects of economic and fiscal performance, may have an even stronger impact. The 1986 federal tax reform will have a profound effect on federal-state-local fiscal balance. Moreover, the reaction by state and local governments to federal policies is shaped by the performance of the U.S. economy. For example, the Carter urban-aid initiatives were enacted in the high inflation/recession years of the mid-1970s and were played out during the time of Propositions 13 and 2½. Surely the state and local government response would have been different if these same programs had been enacted in the more favorable economic climate of the Reagan years.

———————
Roy Bahl is indebted to Wayne Plummer and Loren Williams for assembling the basic data for this paper.

is paper attempts to describe and explain the changing American federalism of the past two decades, taking both the intended and the unintended impacts into account. In the next two sections we describe the basic trends in intergovernmental finance over the past twenty-five years and the changes in the interstate variations in these trends. In the third section, we turn to the question of whether and how these changes might have enhanced or compromised the fiscal condition of state and local governments. The final section speculates about what might become the Bush version of federalism and the changes it could bring during the rest of this century.

Trends in Intergovernmental Finance[1]

The development of the U.S. public sector between 1942 and 1976 can be characterized by three major trends: a growing importance of the federal government sector in the U.S. economy; a shift in public spending toward health, education, and welfare services; and a long-term trend of increase in state and local government dependence on federal intergovernmental transfers.[2] During the past decade, all three of these long term trends have been either bent or reversed.

Growth in the State and Local Government Sector

A reasonable place to begin is to ask whether the state and local government sector has been growing, both relative to the size of the federal sector and as a component of the U.S. economy. By the two most commonly used indicators of government activity—employment and expenditures—it has, at least in recent years. If a public employment benchmark is used, state and local governments have dominated the growth in the public sector in the past twenty years. Public employment may not be an appropriate comparative, however, because the functions of the state and local government sector make it quite labor intensive whereas transfers, debt repayment, capital outlays, and other nonlabor expenditures are much more important at the federal level. Total expenditure, therefore, is probably a better indicator of the relative growth of the state and local sector.

There has been no change in the long term trend of a growing importance of subnational governments in the national economy. The state and local government expenditure share of GNP has increased significantly in the past thirty years. There was a hiatus in this growing

Table 4.1

Government Domestic Expenditure

Calendar year	Percent of total domestic public sector			Percent of GNP		
	Federal[a]	State[b]	Local[c]	Federal[a]	State[b]	Local

From own funds

1954	46.7	24.9	28.2	6.5	3.4	3.9
1964	51.0	23.6	25.3	9.4	4.3	4.6
1974	55.5	25.0	19.5	13.7	6.2	4.8
1981	60.4	23.1	16.5	15.1	5.8	4.1
1982	60.3	23.0	16.7	15.9	6.0	4.4
1983	59.8	22.9	17.3	15.4	5.9	4.5
1984	59.0	23.1	17.9	14.5	5.7	4.4
1985	58.8	23.5	17.7	14.9	6.0	4.4
1986	57.5	24.8	17.7	14.6	6.3	4.5
1987	55.3	25.8	18.9	13.9	6.5	4.8

After intergovernmental transfers[c]

1954	41.1	20.8	37.7	5.7	2.9	5.2
1964	42.3	20.0	37.6	7.8	3.7	6.9
1974	43.4	21.1	35.5	10.8	5.2	8.8
1981	48.9	20.1	31.0	12.3	5.0	7.8
1982	50.2	19.6	30.1	13.2	5.2	7.9
1983	50.0	19.7	30.3	12.9	5.1	7.8
1984	48.9	20.3	30.8	12.0	5.0	7.6
1985	48.9	20.7	30.4	12.4	5.2	7.7
1986	47.8	21.1	31.1	12.1	5.4	7.9
1987	46.4	21.7	31.9	11.7	5.5	8.1

Source: Summarized from various tables in Advisory Committee on Intergovernmental Relations, *Significant Features of Fiscal Federalism*, 1981–82 and 1989 editions (Washington, DC: U.S. Government Printing Office).

[a]Excludes federal expenditure for national defense, international affairs and finance, and space research and technology, and the estimated portion of net interest attributable to these functions. Includes Social Security (OASDHI) and all federal aid to state and local governments, including general revenue sharing payments.

[b] The National Income and Product Accounts do not report state and local government data separately. The state and local expenditure totals (National Income Accounts) were allocated between levels of government on the basis of ratios (by year) reported by the United States Bureau of the Census in the government finance series.

[c]All federal aid to state and local governments, including general revenue sharing payments, is included as state and local expenditure and excluded from federal domestic expenditure.

claim on resources in the early 1980s, but by 1987 the share of GNP had reached 11.3 percent, approximately the level it had reached before Proposition 13 in 1978. The story is somewhat different for the state and local government share of total government expenditures. Federal government domestic expenditures accounted for an increasing share of total public sector activity from the early 1950s until the early 1980s (Table 4.1). Even if defense expenditures are excluded from the computation and intergovernmental transfers are counted as state and local government expenditures, this conclusion holds true.

This pattern was reversed in the 1980s, and the state and local government share of public expenditures (after transfers) has risen from 49.7 percent in 1982 to 53.6 percent in 1987. The break in the general pattern that seems to have occurred in recent years is an important turnaround, especially in light of how the tax limitation movement of the late 1970s suppressed tax increases by state and local governments. The Advisory Commission on Intergovernmental Relations (ACIR) estimated that none of the $30 billion in real state-tax increase during 1976–80 was due to political actions,[3] and the ratio of state and local government taxes to personal income fell from 12.8 percent in 1977 to 11.6 percent in 1982. Beginning with a 1983 round of state government tax increases, largely in response to the economic slowdown and federal aid reductions during 1981–83, the growth in spending and revenue raising shifted back to the state and local government sector and the average rate of taxation increased. Though the level of state and local government taxes still has not risen past its 1978 level, the turnaround in its revenue raising efforts is impressive. Though the federal government is nearly twice as large in terms of tax collections, state and local governments have accounted for half of all tax collections since 1980.[4]

There are a number of possible explanations for this stronger state and local government fiscal performance: the discretionary response to federal aid cutbacks and the retrenchment in federal domestic programs, the unleashing of public sector demands that were held in check during the limitation years, and the combination of the natural buoyancy of state government revenue systems and the strong performance of the economy.

Increased Social Welfare Expenditures

A second dominant trend in the U.S. fiscal system has been the continuing increase in the budget claim of health, education, and welfare expendi-

Table 4.2

Sources of Growth in Federal Domestic Expenditures

	Percent distribution of social welfare expenditures			Percent of GNP		
Calendar year	Social Security (OASDHI)[a]	Federal aid[b]	All other[c]	Social Security (OASDHI)[a]	Federal aid[b]	All other[c]
1954	15.4	11.7	72.9	1.0	0.8	4.7
1964	27.1	16.6	56.3	2.5	1.6	5.3
1974	35.8	21.5	42.7	4.9	2.9	5.9
1981	40.2	18.7	41.1	6.1	2.8	6.2
1982	41.6	16.4	42.0	6.6	2.6	6.7
1983	42.9	16.1	41.0	6.6	2.5	6.3
1984	44.1	16.8	39.0	6.4	2.4	5.6
1985	43.4	16.4	40.2	6.4	2.4	6.0
1986	44.3	16.8	38.9	6.5	2.5	5.7
1987	45.4	15.7	38.8	6.4	2.2	5.5

Source: Summarized from Advisory Commission on Intergovernmental Relations (ACIR), *Significant Features*, 1981–82, and 1989 editions, various tables.

[a]National Income and Product Account.

[b]Federal aid as reported in the National Income Accounts (used here) differs slightly from the federal payments (census) series (used in Table 4.3). The major difference is the inclusion of federal payments for low-rent public housing (estimated at $3.5 billion in 1980) in the census series but excluded by definition from the NIA series. Federal general revenue sharing is included in both series.

[c]Includes direct federal expenditure for education, public assistance and relief, veterans benefits and services, commerce, transportation, and housing, and others.

tures. The postwar increase in public expenditures at all levels of government, as well as the shift toward an increasing federal share, has been largely due to increased social welfare expenditures.[5]

At the federal level, the expenditure increases of the 1960s and 1970s were dominated by Social Security expenditures and grants to state and local governments (Table 4.2). The Social Security share of federal domestic expenditures more than doubled between 1954 and 1980, and the amount of federal aid to state and local governments doubled between 1954 and 1978, increasing as a share of federal domestic expenditures from 11.7 percent in 1954 to 18.7 percent in 1981. Moreover, there was a marked shift toward social welfare services in the composition of this federal aid.

Again, there would appear to be a structural break in recent years. Assistance to state and local governments as a share of the total federal budget has been declining since 1978 and though the Social Security share of expenditures has not fallen, its share of GNP has not increased. As a share of GNP, social welfare expenditures were lower in 1987 than they were in 1981.

The reversal has been much more dramatic at the state and local government level. About 60 percent of the expenditure increase during the 1960–76 period was for health, education, and welfare purposes, but this share fell to 56 percent between 1976 and 1981. Put another way, the average 1 percent increase in GNP between 1960 and 1976 generated a 1.56 percent increase in social welfare expenditures. Between 1976 and 1981, this income elasticity of social welfare expenditures was only 0.84. During the 1982–86 growth period, the average 1 percent increase in personal income was associated with only a 0.95 percent increase in health, education, and welfare expenditures by state and local governments.

The implications of these elasticities are not as clear as one would like. One explanation is that federal assistance to state and local governments and direct federal expenditures for health, education, and welfare purposes, have been cut. On average, state and local governments have responded relatively more by passing these cuts along to beneficiaries than by raising taxes or redirecting expenditures from other areas. However, the fact is that state and local governments did raise revenues during this period by enough to offset the federal aid reductions. Another explanation, then, is that citizens were demanding a reduction in the share of their personal income spent on social welfare activities. However, there is much variation in this pattern and it is difficult to isolate a clear national pattern.[6]

Federal Aid Dependence

The third major trend of the past two decades has been the growing importance of federal aid flows in the public sector. For every 1 percent increase in GNP between 1954 and 1976, federal general revenues (including Social Security) grew by about 1 percent, state and local government revenues from own sources by about 2 percent, and federal aid by about 5 percent. With this trend came a growing reliance by state and local governments on federal aid. By 1978, federal aid accounted for 22 percent of total state and local government revenue and was a more

Table 4.3

Reliance of State and Local Government on Federal Aid and Major Tax Revenue Sources

	Percent of total general revenue			
Year	Federal aid	Property taxes	Income taxes	Sales taxes[a]
1954	10.3	34.4	6.6	25.1
1964	14.7	31.0	8.0	23.1
1974	20.1	23.0	12.3	22.2
1976	21.7	22.3	12.3	21.3
1977	21.9	21.9	13.4	21.2
1978	22.0	21.0	13.9	21.4
1979	21.8	18.9	14.3	21.6
1980	21.7	17.9	14.5	20.9
1981	21.3	17.7	14.3	20.3
1982	19.1	18.0	14.4	20.5
1983	18.5	18.3	14.3	20.6
1984	17.9	17.8	15.0	21.0
1985	17.8	17.4	14.9	21.1
1986	17.6	17.4	14.7	21.0
1987	16.6	17.7	15.5	21.0

Source: U.S. Bureau of the Census, *Governmental Finances*, Series GF No. 5 (Washington, DC: U.S. Government Printing Office, various years).
[a]Includes general and selective sales taxes.

important financing source than any of the property, sales, or income taxes (Table 4.3).

Since the late 1970s, federal grants declined in importance as a financing source for state and local governments, reversing a two-decade trend of increase. The National Income Accounts (NIA) show that at the end of 1987 the federal financing share had fallen to 16.6 percent of state and local government revenues.[7] By 1987, state and local governments were raising as much from the property tax as they were receiving in federal aid (Table 4.3).

Increasing Centralization

Accompanying these three important trends has been a growing dominance of state government within the state and local sector. The state

Table 4.4

Indicators of Fiscal Importance: Means and Interstate Variation

	Total expenditures as percent of state personal income				Federal aid as percent of personal income				Revenues from own source as percent of personal income				State government percent of direct expenditures				State government percent of tax revenues			
	1967	1977	1982	1987	1967	1977	1982	1987	1967	1977	1982	1987	1967	1977	1982	1987	1967	1977	1982	1987
Mean	18.6	18.6	21.3	22.5	3.4	4.6	3.7	3.5	12.7	14.7	16.0	16.6	44.3	44.4	45.0	45.8	56.8	62.4	64.5	63.8
Coefficient of variation	0.21	0.16	0.25	0.31	0.62	0.26	0.25	0.31	0.14	0.18	0.59	0.36	0.23	0.21	0.20	0.19	0.20	0.17	0.16	0.15

Source: U.S. Bureau of the Census, *Governmental Finances* (Washington, DC: U.S. Government Printing Office, various years).

government share of total taxes collected rose from 57 to 65 percent between 1967 and 1982, though the states' share of direct expenditures remained approximately constant during this period (see Table 4.4).[8]

There are a number of explanations for this trend. One—widely believed, but not supported by these data—is that state government income and sales taxes are more buoyant than local property taxes, and there was a substantial growth in real income. Another is that state governments increased assistance to locally provided services in some cases, and directly assumed service responsibilities in others, largely to forestall politically unpopular increases in the effective rate of property taxation. Yet another possibility is that the states were better able to look after themselves with discretionary changes in sales and income tax rates than were local governments who had to rely on the property tax—another manifestation of John Shannon's "fend-for-yourself federalism." Whatever the reason, this trend was interrupted in the 1980s and there has been no significant change in the state government share of taxes. It is important to note that these are aggregate data and describe the importance of state vs. local government as sectors of the economy. As we show below, wide interstate variations lie beneath this average behavior.

Interstate Variations

The data in Tables 4.1–4.4 tell a story that the pattern of intergovernmental finance has changed in the 1980s. Some longstanding trends—most notably the growing importance of the state and local government sector in the economy—have continued. Other trends have been broken in the 1980s suggesting some very important changes in the system. The responsibility for revenue raising has shifted from the federal to the state-local sector but within the state-local sector the strong trend toward state fiscal centralization may have stopped. Revenue effort by state and local governments has increased since the early 1980s to make up for federal aid reductions, and there has been a shift away from spending for social services at all levels of government. As may be seen from Table 4.4, there is a trend toward uniformity among the states in some of these trends, e.g., increased state responsibility for expenditures and revenue raising, but much less uniformity in most of the other dimensions of fiscal change reported.[9] This suggests the need to examine more closely the interstate variations in fiscal performance.

Five dimensions of the interstate variation are considered here: (a) the increasing fiscal centralization to the state government level, (b) changes in the rate of revenue mobilization, (c) the declines in federal aid, (d) the determinants of variations in state and local government expenditures, and (e) the changing structure of state and local government revenues and expenditures.

Fiscal Centralization

As reported in Tables 4.1 and 4.4, the 1980s have seen a shift in revenue raising power to the state and local government level but an interruption of the growing fiscal dominance of state governments. Average tax revenue centralization in the 1967–77 period increased substantially (Table 4.4) and most states centralized their revenue systems (Table 4.5). The 1977–87 period again shows more states centralizing than decentralizing their revenue-raising powers, but during this period there was no increase in the aggregate share of taxes collected at the state government level. It is significant to note, however, that only five states increased the share of own-source revenues raised at the local level during the 1977–87 period. The trend toward centralization is less evident on the expenditure side during the 1967–77 period. The average state government share of expenditures rose only slightly and twenty-five states centralized their expenditure responsibility while only twelve decentralized. Though there was no appreciable change in the aggregate state-local expenditure share between 1977 and 1987, twenty-three states decentralized while only fourteen centralized.

Revenue Mobilization

On average, state and local government revenues raised from own sources increased from 14.7 percent of personal income in 1977 to 16.6 percent in 1987 (Table 4.6). However, when Alaska is removed from the comparison, there appears to have been little increase in the average state and local government revenue burden over the past decade. There have, however, been substantial interstate variations in revenue mobilization, and the question we raise here is the extent to which these trends are uniform and the kinds of states that have gone with and against the trend.

There was no significant correlation between the revenue mobilization ratio and per-capita income in 1967 or in 1987, but in 1977 (immediately

Table 4.5

Trends in Fiscal Centralization in State and Local Government

	Number of states with		
	increased centralization[a]	increased decentralization	no change
Revenues			
1967–77	26	13	11
1977–87	27	7	16
Expenditures			
1967–77	25	14	11
1977–87	14	23	13

[a]*Increased fiscal centralization* is defined as an increase in the ratio of state to state and local government revenues raised from own sources of more than two percentage points. *Decentralization* refers to a decline of more than two percentage points. *Expenditure decentralization* is defined in an analogous way.

after the recession) high-income states were mobilizing a significantly greater revenue share. This finding for the post-1975 recession period is consistent with the Advisory Commission on Intergovernmental Relations' (ACIR) observation that states experiencing fiscal stress will be the ones who increase tax effort,[10] and with the fact that many higher income states were hardest hit by that recession. The 1980s, Gold and Zelio note, has been more of a case of low taxing (and lower income) states catching up.[11] In all years, however, states which mobilized a greater share of personal income in revenues received a significantly greater level of per capita federal grants. States in all four census regions, on average, moved with this general trend.

Declining Federal Aid

A policy event of major importance in the late 1970s and early 1980s has been the substantial slowing of growth in federal grants to state and local governments. Inflation-adjusted federal grant revenues fell from $49.4 billion in 1978 to an estimated $37.7 billion in 1987; from 3.7 to 2.2

Table 4.6

Revenue Mobilization

	1967	1977	1987
Revenue share[a]			
Average	12.7	14.7	16.6
Range	7.8	16.3	41.3
Highest	17.3 (ND)	20.6 (NY)[b]	31.7 (WY)[b]
Lowest	9.6 (IL)	11.7 (MO)	11.66 (NH)
Regional average revenue shares			
North	11.4	15.0	15.0
South	12.1	13.3	15.0
Midwest	12.7	14.5	15.4
West	14.5	16.6	20.7
Correlations with revenue share			
Per capita income			
Per capita federal grants			

[a]Revenue from own sources as a percentage of personal income.
[b]Excluding Alaska, which ranked first.

percent of GNP. The result is that state and local governments have become much less dependent on federal aid: from 22 percent of total general revenues in 1978, federal assistance dropped below 17 percent in 1987 (Table 4.3).

In real terms, per capita federal aid did not grow at all over the 1977–87 period, by comparison with an average increase of $112 between 1967 and 1977 (see Table 4.7). The federal aid declines of the last decade were widespread, taking place in twenty-two states.

Is there a pattern to the retrenchment in federal aid? As may be seen in Table 4.7, there is no significant correlation between changes in real per capita federal aid and changes in real per capita income between 1977 and 1987. However, this is different from the situation in the previous decade. In the 1967–77 period, states which experienced greater increases in per capita income experienced greater increases in per capita federal aid. At the margin, the system was counterequalizing.

It may be instructive to point out how some states escaped the most severe consequences of the federal aid retrenchment. New York state, for example, has suffered less than much of the rest of the nation.[12] For

Table 4.7

Trends in Federal Assistance

	1967–77	1977–87
Change in per capita federal aid		
in current dollars	152	180
in real 1982 dollars	112	0
Regional averages (in real 1982 dollars)		
North	190	29
South	108	6
Midwest	120	30
West	57	–54
Number of states with real declines	4	22
Correlation of change in per capita federal aid with change in per capita income	0.629	0.024

all New York state and local governments combined, the share of total U.S. federal aid rose from 10.1 percent in 1970 to 11.3 percent in 1984, despite the fact that New York's per capita income level has remained above average and its share of national population has declined. New York City's share of total direct federal aid to local governments also increased, from 6.1 to 7.2 percent over the same period. Since 1980, the rate of increase in real federal aid to New York state and local governments also has been above the national average. While real federal aid declined nationally, it actually increased in New York. There was a real decline in New York City, but it was only about one-third of that for all local governments in the nation. As a result of this pattern, the dependency of New York state and local governments on federal grants rose above the national average. New York City's dependency is down from a high of 7.9 percent of general revenues in 1980, but has been increasing since 1982.

The composition of federal aid to the New York state government has continued to change markedly toward public welfare: such aid accounted for 69 percent of the total in 1984 versus 57 percent in 1980. (The comparable figures for the U.S. are 47 percent and 40 percent.) In fact, New York State received nearly 17 percent of all federal aid for public welfare. By contrast, highway and education aid are declining in real terms in New York, and the state's national shares are down markedly.

In sum, New York's governments have avoided some of the consequences of federal aid retrenchment because of their claims on federal welfare spending. Will this continue? If not, will the state and city make up for the revenue loss? In all likelihood, real reductions in aid will continue as the federal government "offloads" part of its deficit on to state and local government. Proposed welfare reforms almost certainly would reinforce this trend. Finally, it is doubtful that a state with a per capita income 14 percent above the national average and a population equivalent to about 7.5 percent of the national population can sustain an 11.4 percent share of total federal aid. Sooner or later there will be pressure to bring the New York share into line with its population share and its financial capacity. Future declines in population share, and thus in New York's congressional representation, are important considerations in this regard.

Expenditure Determinants

State and local government per capita expenditures in 1986 vary from highs (excluding Alaska) of $4,966 and $4,324 in Wyoming and New York, to lows of $2,085 and $2,165 in Arkansas and Missouri. Public-policy analysts have long been interested in the study of determinants of this variation, and much empirical and theoretical work has been done.[13] The results of the empirical studies tend to square with economic theory and a significant portion of the interstate variation in per capita expenditures can be explained.

In this paper, no attempt is made to develop a new theoretical model. Rather, we want to answer two simple questions: (a) to what extent are interstate variations in the level of per capita expenditures associated with differences in per capita income, population, and land area and how has this relationship changed over the years; and (b) has the relationship between per capita federal grants and per capita expenditures, holding constant income, population, and land area, changed in the past two decades?

The results of a regression analysis, designed to answer these questions, are presented in Table 4.8. The response of per capita expenditures to per capita income is positive and significant in all years and the regression coefficients are remarkably stable. Land area shows a positive

Table 4.8

Ordinary Least Squares Estimates of the Determinants of Per Capita State and Local Government Expenditures[a]

	1967		1977		1987	
	Without federal grants	With federal grants	Without federal grants	With federal grants	Without federal grants	With federal grants
Constant	-277.0179 (2.13)	-95.7313 (1.20)	-555.3443 (1.76)	-952.1954 (5.62)	-695.3042 (1.44)	-2,056.9587 (7.10)
Per capita income	0.2182 (16.11)	0.1231 (9.44)	0.2356 (7.04)	0.1716 (9.28)	0.2098 (6.10)	0.1804 (9.61)
Population	-0.0324 (3.59)	0.0060 (0.89)	-0.0230 (2.45)	0.0013 (0.23)	-0.0587 (3.73)	-0.0328 (3.71)
Land area	0.0017 (3.68)	-0.0004 (1.23)	0.0023 (4.29)	0.0007 (2.24)	0.0104 (11.49)	0.0073 (12.87)
Per capita federal grants	—	2.2561 (9.25)	—	2.2809 (11.04)	—	4.4685 (10.61)
R^2	0.84	0.94	0.71	0.92	0.77	0.93

[a] t-statistic shown in parentheses below the regression coefficent.

coefficient reflecting the higher cost of serving a more dispersed population and the high fixed cost of providing certain services. The coefficients are significant in all years. Population size is negatively related to per capita expenditures, holding constant land area and income, suggesting that larger urban agglomerations, *ceteris paribus*, may offer some economies of size. There is little change in the population regression coefficients over this time period. In short, the determinants of interstate variations in public expenditures have not changed much over the past twenty years.

In a second set of equations, federal aid has been added as a right side variable. The relationship with per capita expenditures is positive and significant, and the coefficient is larger in 1987 than in 1967. The hazards of such estimation with ordinary least squares (OLS) are widely known: a least squares bias since the dependent variable may be a determinant of the level of grants received, a specification error in the overall equation since many variables other than income, population, and land determine expenditure levels, and multicollinearity between the grant and other explanatory variables. Even so, many have argued that OLS estimates do give a reasonable approximation of the association between grants and expenditure. These results do not suggest that the stimulative impact of grants is any smaller in the 1980s than it was in the 1970s. States that receive larger amounts of federal grants, on average, spend significantly more.

The Structure of Revenue and Expenditures

There have been decided shifts in the structure of revenues and expenditures. In the past decade federal grants have declined in importance as a financing source and local revenues have increased to pick up some of the shortfall (Table 4.9). However, all state and local government revenues did not increase to the same degree. In fact, revenues from the traditional broad-based state and local government taxes declined from 9.6 percent of GNP in 1978 to 8.8 percent in 1986. The real increase in state and local government revenues has come from a mixture of selective sales taxes, user charges, lotteries, interest income, royalties, and a broad assortment of licenses. In terms of the change in the mix of taxes, there were some consistencies among the states. It is interesting to note that no state increased its property tax share of total revenues or its federal aid share of total revenues between 1977 and 1987.

Table 4.9

Changing Revenue and Expenditure Composition

	1967	1977	Number of states with increasing shares 1967–77	1987	Number of states with increasing shares 1977–87
Percent of own source general revenues					
Property tax	31.7	26.0	3	20.6	0
Sales tax	27.3	16.3	1	16.4	25
Income tax	7.2	15.0	46	15.7	28
Federal aid	26.2	31.3	43	21.7	0
Other	33.7	42.6	48	47.3	41
State aid as a percent of total state and local government expenditure	15.1	19.0	44	15.6	6
Percent of expenditures					
Education	37.1	38.8	34	30.8	0
Welfare	7.3	10.6	46	9.6	13
Health	5.6	8.0	45	7.0	12
Highways	16.4	11.0	0	8.2	6
Other	33.6	31.6	18	44.4	50

During this same period, there was a significant change in the distribution of state and local government expenditure budgets across functions. Between 1967 and 1977, thirty-four states increased their budget share on education and as a result about 1.7 cents more of every revenue dollar went for education. Since 1977, no state has increased its share of expenditures for education and about 8 cents less of each revenue dollar is now spent on education. The average shares spent on health, welfare, and highways also dropped in the 1977–87 period and relatively few states moved against this trend.

State Aid to Local Governments

State intergovernmental expenditures increased to a new high in 1987, $141 billion, compared to $132 billion in 1986 and $108 billion in 1984.[14] As a percentage of state government general expenditure, state intergovernmental payments have remained approximately constant at about 35 percent in the 1980s. However, as a percent of total state and local government expenditure, state aid has declined in the 1980s (Table 4.9). The average per capita amount of state aid was $583 in 1987, with thirty-nine states falling between $350 and $800. Two states spent more than $1,000 per capita in state aid payments: Alaska ($1,785) and Wyoming ($1,122). Hawaii has per capita aid payments of $40 and New Hampshire $172. These variations reflect different choices in terms of the assignment of responsibility to state vs. local governments, rather than any underfinancing or overfinancing of the local government sector. For example, the low per capita aid figure in Hawaii is mostly a reflection of state government operation of the local education system.

Education still receives by far the greatest share of state aid to local governments (about 62 percent) and welfare is second with 12 percent. However, nine states administer their welfare programs directly so no major welfare aid payments are made by these states to local governments. Both the education and welfare shares of state aid have remained approximately constant in the 1980s. General local government support received 10 percent of total 1987 state aid payments and this share has been fairly constant since 1978, as has the 4.8 percent of all state aid allocated to highways.

Fiscal Conditions[15]

This reading of the data brings us to the conclusion that the state and local government sector is being pushed to a position of greater fiscal self-sufficiency and the governments have responded by increasing their rate of revenue mobilization, and by changing the orientation of their budgets and methods of financing. Does this reaction give rise to a new fiscal strength or to a fiscal weakness in the state and local government sector? Does the unevenness in the response of state and local governments suggest that the fiscal condition of certain types of governments has been compromised by federal policy?

The most used (and oftentimes the most misused) measure of fiscal condition is the general surplus of state and local governments as reported in the National Income Accounts (NIA). An increase in the surplus—a measure of the excess of current revenues over total expenditures (excluding social insurance funds)—may result because of economic growth or increased government efficiency, but one may also reach a larger surplus by raising taxes to exorbitant levels, carrying larger cash balances, reducing essential expenditure or deferring infrastructure maintenance.[16] Still, the general surplus probably does indicate how state and local governments adjust their budgetary policies in response to the economic environment and provides some indirect evidence about whether there has been a change in state and local government policy in the 1980s. Our specific questions are whether the size of the surplus, the determinants of its variation and its cyclical sensitivity are different in the 1980s as compared with the 1970s.

The large surplus in recent years, as reported in Table 4.10, is seen by some as indication of an unusually strong fiscal position of state and local governments. There was a positive general account surplus from the second quarter of 1983 until the fourth quarter of 1986. During this period, the surplus averaged $13.9 billion (in constant 1982 dollars) and 2.8 percent of state and local government expenditures. A surplus of this magnitude suggests that state and local governments had ample discretionary funds with which to support public service levels and to compensate for the loss of federal funds. The question arises as to whether the size of this surplus is abnormally large by comparison with the 1970s, whether it has been less cyclical, and whether the determinants of variations in its size were different in the 1980s.

In fact, the maximum level of the surplus in the 1980s, relative to either total state and local government expenditures or to GNP, has not exceeded the high levels achieved during expansion periods in the 1970s. What is different is that state and local governments have maintained large surpluses over longer periods of time in the 1980s.

Table 4.10

General Account Surplus of State and Local Government Trends and Cyclical Swing

Year: quarter	(peak/trough)[a]	Amount (billons, 1982 dollars)[b]	Percent of total expenditures
1970:IV	(trough)	−18.7	−5.32
1972:IV	(peak)	28.6	7.57
1975:I	(trough)	−20.2	−5.07
1977:III	(peak)	19.5	4.73
1980:II	(trough)	−4.0	−0.95
1981:III	(peak)	6.5	1.55
1983:I	(trough)	−3.9	−0.93
1984:II	(peak)	21.1	4.90
1988:II		−9.0	−1.79

Cycle[c]	Cyclical swing (in billions)		Net accumulation (in billions)	
	current dollars	1982 dollars[b]	current dollars	1982 dollars[b]
1969:III–1973:IV	5.8	13.9	−2.1	−8.0
1973:IV–1980:I	8.3	13.6	8.6	7.9
1980:I–1981:III	6.9	7.7	3.5	3.7
1981:III–1988:II[d]	5.2	4.9	27.1	25.5

Sources: Computed from U.S. Department of Commerce, Bureau of Economic Analysis, *National Income and Product Accounts, 1929–82, and Survey of Current Business,* July 1986, 1987, and 1988, and September 1988.

[a]Peak and trough in terms of the size of the real general account surplus.
[b]Deflated using the implicit GNP deflator for state and local government purchases.
[c]From the beginning of one contraction to the end of the following expansion.
[d]The latest data available at the time of this writing.

The general surplus as a percent of expenditures averaged 0.7 percent during the 1975–80 expansion compared to 1.6 percent in the present expansion. Similarly, the deficits during the 1981–82 contraction were much smaller than those in past contractions—an average of 0.1 percent during 1981–82—versus 2.4 percent in 1973–74. This means that state and local governments have had a greater opportunity to accumulate fiscal resources during the 1980s. It is this long expansion that may have helped state and local governments withstand the federal aid reductions without substantial tax increases. The condition of every state and local government is not strong but the sector as a whole appears to be doing better in the 1980s than it did in the 1970s.

Another dimension of fiscal health is stability. The surplus is known to be cyclical—it falls during contractions and rises during expansions. Has it reacted more or less to the business cycles of the 1980s? We have calculated a cyclical swing in the general surplus, i.e., the difference in the average quarterly general surplus in a contraction and that in the following expansion. The greater the swing, the more sensitive the surplus is to a particular business cycle. For example, the average quarterly surplus swung from a negative $4.58 billion during the 1969–70 contraction to a positive $1.19 billion during the 1970–73 expansion for a swing of $5.77 billion during the 1969–73 cycle (Table 4.10). The results of computing these swings in real terms for all business cycles in the 1970s and 1980s leads to the conclusion that the surplus has been markedly less cyclical in the 1980s.

This is consistent with the hypothesis that the 1980s brought a more conservative fiscal behavior on the part of state and local governments. The painful lessons learned in the 1970s almost certainly made state and local governments more risk averse, and many of the frills were trimmed away from budgets. The increased use of general contingency funds in the 1980s and significant discretionary increases in taxes in response to the 1981–82 recession indicated an attempt by state and local governments to stabilize their fiscal condition.[17] As emphasized by John Shannon, state and local governments could not count on a federal bailout during the recession as in the 1970s, so they had to respond quickly on their own.[18] Risk aversion also forced state and local governments to build their expectations about the macroeconomy into their fiscal planning: a better job of prediction may have been done, and improved accounting and performance budgeting systems have made better expenditure control possible. The result is that even some central cities, the hardest pressed segment of the local government structure, were recording positive general fund balances in the mid-1980s. Dearborn concluded that large cities were "in perhaps the best financial condition they have been in since 1971, as judged by their success in balancing budgets and maintaining balance sheet surpluses and liquidity."[19]

The Response to Bush Federalism

The Bush administration's version of fiscal federalism is not yet known.

Yet, one can speculate about three policy areas where state and local government finances will be significantly affected during the time of this administration. The most important—a legacy of the Reagan program— is the longer-run reaction of state and local governments to the 1986 tax reform, which we argue here will slow the growth in the state and local government sector. The other two are areas where policies of the new administration will have an impact on the fiscal balance among the federal, state, and local government sectors. The deficit will likely encourage a continuation of the policy of no real growth in federal grants, which will reinforce the tax reform in encouraging a smaller state and local government sector. Finally, the deficit may force the administration to propose further tax policy changes such as removing deductibility for state and local government income and property taxes, increasing the effective marginal personal income tax rate, or enacting a national sales tax. Any of these policies could have important effects on the role of the state and local government sector in the public financing system.

The 1986 Tax Reform

The new tax code was never intended to influence the federal structure, but it well may cause state and local governments to adjust their thinking about how they should tax as well as how much they can afford to spend and borrow. The fact is that the federal tax reform could activate or accelerate a chain of other events: possible reductions in state aid; heightened fiscal competition between the city and its suburbs; impacts on the poor; stimulation of investment in the service sector; and changes in personal tax burdens. The features of the tax reform that will be responsible for these impacts include (a) elimination of deductibility for passive real estate losses and sales taxes, (b) reduction in the marginal tax rate, and (c) elimination of certain tax preferences for capital intensive, goods producing industries.

City-Suburban Competition

One consequence of federal tax reform will be increased city-suburban competition for a smaller pool of state grant money. This will come about because of slower natural growth in state revenues, which will depress state aid, and an increase in the relative price of suburban property taxes. Consider first the prospects for a slower growth in state government revenues. Elimination of sales tax deductibility and reduction in the federal marginal tax rate will raise the price of state and local government taxes for those who itemize deductions.[20] Itemizer-voters may react to this by demanding lower state taxes. Research does not provide a clear answer about how great this reaction might be. Gramlich's[21] analysis suggests that it may be small; Kenyon[22] and Inman[23] find an effect on income but not sales taxes; and Feldstein and Metcalf [24] estimate a positive response from combined personal taxes on income, consumption and property values. Assume, as seems reasonable, that the longer-run growth in state sales and income taxes will be less than would have been the case if the marginal federal tax rate had not been lowered. With a slower growth in taxes, and with further cutbacks in federal aid, it is likely that the revenue pool available from which to draw state aid to local governments will be smaller in the future than it would otherwise have been. History has shown the state aid share of total state government expenditures to remain approximately constant, hence we might expect under this scenario to have lower state aid than otherwise would have been the case.

The other side of this story is that the competition for this reduced pool of state aid will be more keen. As state aid is reduced, pressure will build on the local property tax to pick up some of the slack. This will be resisted by industrial taxpayers, particularly because some capital-intensive firms will have experienced a significant tax increase due to the 1986 reform. Suburban residents, who have higher incomes and are more likely to itemize, will lose some of the federal subsidy to their property tax bill. Their property tax will have risen. It is almost certain that these voters will resist tax increases designed to compensate for federal aid reductions, and they will look to the state capitol for relief in the form of increased school aid. Such proposals are not likely to fall on deaf ears in the suburban-dominated state legislature. Cities, whose residents do not suffer as much directly from the loss of deductibility and the lower marginal tax rates, may not fare well in such a competition. Moreover, if the increased state aids are funded from cuts in social programs, city residents will be doubly damned.

How might this situation be avoided, that is, how might the potential revenue reductions be covered? Consider the possibilities: (a) increased federal aid; (b) increased growth rates in state and city economies; (c) increased sales, income, or property tax rates; and (d) retrenchment. The first seems highly unlikely. The second will occur in some places but not others. The third seems improbable, especially for states that are already in a noncompetitive taxing position, because the "price" of tax increases is now higher, and because some states have just taken a major step in the direction of lowering income taxes. Expenditure reductions and heightened city-suburban competition for a smaller pool of state aid are almost certain to result.

Impacts on Cities' Taxable Capacity

Federal tax reform also will affect the strength of central city economies and the ability of city tax systems to draw on it. Not only do reductions in the real growth of federal and state aid seem certain, but federal tax reform may lead to a dampening of the growth in taxes raised by city governments. Why? First, because the higher effective price of sales, income, and property taxes will heighten taxpayer resistance. Second, the lower marginal tax rate and the disallowance of passive real estate losses are provisions of the tax reform that will reduce implicit subsidies to both housing consumption and investment.[25] On the consumption side, this may reduce the demand for home ownership among itemizers which, in turn, will depress the growth in real estate values and the property tax base. On the investment side, the removal of tax preferences for new plants and equipment may discourage new construction. These impacts are especially important because the growth in the property tax base and yield are more heavily dependent on new construction than on reassessment.

There is, potentially, a brighter side of the tax reform story for the economy of large core cities. The new tax code removes an investment subsidy that has benefited manufacturers who make disproportionately heavy investments in plant and equipment. As a result, the relative profitability of investments in the service sector, including finance, will increase. This should help urban governments whose economies are concentrated in the service sector: for example, services now constitute about 45 percent of New York City employment compared to only 11 percent in manufacturing.

From the point of view of manufacturers, especially the most capital intensive, federal tax reform will discourage investment in plant and equipment. That is bad news for cities that still rely heavily on a manufacturing base. One could argue that the new code will further shake the already weak competitive position of many capital intensive, goods-producing firms. The long term effects are difficult to analyze.

Interstate Competition and Expenditure Reductions

In high taxing states, it seems clear that the tax burden disparity with the rest of the nation is potentially widened by federal tax reform. One study estimated the overall impact as follows: while high-income New York City residents would see a 5 percent tax increase, comparable families in New Jersey and Connecticut will see a 4 percent reduction.[26] Moreover, lower taxing states, those with fewer itemizers, and those without income taxes will improve their competitive position.

Federal aid reductions and the reduction in the federal tax subsidy will force all states to rely more heavily on their own financing. This suggests that states will be more hesitant to let their tax rates drift "out of line," particularly those that already are relatively high. In fact, one view is that more than ever before, states and cities will compete for jobs using fiscal incentives.[27]

To the extent that economic development objectives will drive state fiscal policies more than they presently do, distribution of income through the public sector may suffer.[28] This is because such policies are likely to be neither pro-urban nor pro-poor. Tax incentives to attract industry will be focused on company tax "holidays" or reduced tax rates, industrial and commercial property tax forgiveness, and a reduction in the top marginal personal income tax rates. There also will be pressure to reduce taxes on certain types of businesses to compensate for federal tax increases. On the expenditure side, the story is much the same. Industrial subsidies to attract plant location and general improvements in infrastructure will be leading candidates for inclusion in state or local government industrial policy. Education services may also play a role, likely in the direction of improving technical training or the general education system in the state.

Suppose a state were to follow such a strategy of competitive industrial subsidies? What are the implications for its public finances? Lower state taxes mean less direct state spending and less state aid for urban programs. Industrial policy type reforms may also reduce the built-in elasticity of the income tax. Consider the case of New York which enacted reforms in 1987 that cut the level of taxes and reduced the built-in elasticity of the income tax, i.e., its potential revenue response to future income growth. This reinforces the tendency for a slower growing state and local government sector. Finally, the tax structure changes implied for such an economic development program (income tax and business property tax reductions) reduce the progressivity of the tax system.

The other side of the story is that the right industrial policy programs might stimulate job growth in cities. The problem here is that central city employment in much of the nation is growing relatively slowly, indicating that the city's business climate is not competitive and will not share fully in a successful state industrial policy. As for the effect of employment growth on alleviation of urban poverty, it is clear that even low-paying service sector jobs are not a good match for the lowest income unemployed in central cities.[29]

Effects on Poor People

Another way to view tax reform is in terms of its effect on people, and especially on the poor. The urban poor are not affected directly by federal tax reform since, in general, they do not pay income taxes. Thus they will receive no more take-home pay as a result of lower federal rates, and they would pay no more if the state government kept the windfall. Actually, the urban poor might fare better in the short run if the windfall were spent on human capital development in inner cities.

More important are the indirect effects on the urban poor. We can but speculate about these. One scenario is that the long-run income elasticity of the reformed federal income tax (and state income taxes) will be lower, suggesting a lower revenue yield relative to GNP in the future. If national income growth slows, even greater federal aid cuts will be forced. These cuts may be borne heavily by the social programs. State aid and direct expenditures for the poor also could suffer because of removal of the federal deductibility subsidy and because of interstate and interlocal fiscal competition. In addition there may be less rental housing construction and a drift toward higher rents, both factors that compromise the real income position of the urban poor.

The more optimistic view is that the federal reforms will stimulate growth in the U.S. economy and that the urban poor will share in this growth. The possibility that the job growth in the city will capture the urban poor, however, may be wishful thinking. The events of the past decade seem to make it clear that those living in poverty are not likely to share in the employment benefits of a stronger national economic growth. It is also argued that increased jobs in the service sector will not improve the lot of the lowest income residents in the central city. Indeed, some have argued that service jobs do not "fit" the urban poorest, and may even exacerbate the unemployment problem.[30]

Possible New Structural Reforms

The solution to the federal budget deficit problem will almost certainly lead to some form of tax increase in the future. If the decision is made to raise the additional funds through income taxation, then two likely avenues of reform are a temporary income tax surrate and a reduction in tax expenditures such as, perhaps, deductibility of state and local government income and property taxes. While both of these measures will work in the direction of increasing federal revenues, it is not clear how they will effect the revenue raising decisions of state and local governments.

On the one hand, an increase in the marginal tax rate will reduce the after-federal-tax purchasing power of citizens, and therefore will erode the base which state and local governments tax. On the other hand, the higher marginal tax rate will increase the value of deductibility of income and property taxes and therefore will reduce the price of state and local government taxes. This will have the effect, all other things being the same, of removing some of the disincentive to increased state and local government taxation.

If the federal government were to move in the direction of broadening the federal income tax base by reducing certain tax expenditures, property tax and income tax deductibility would be a likely target. If deductibility were eliminated, or even reduced for these two taxes, the result would be to drive up the tax price for those who itemize deductions. The result would be an increased resistance to higher state and local government taxes and quite likely some pressure to lower the effective tax rate.

Conclusions

It is too soon to make a definitive argument that a permanent shift in the nature of American federalism has occurred in the 1980s. But the trends have clearly been bent. The new movement is toward fiscal decentralization, the passing down to subnational governments of the responsibility for a greater share of taxing and spending decisions. The state and local government share of total government direct expenditures and revenue responsibility has been increasing in the 1980s, reversing a longstanding trend of growing federal fiscal dominance, and the sector share of GNP increased during the 1980–87 time period. At the same time, the dependence on federal grants has declined dramatically and grant conditionality has been eased, giving local governments more discretion over what they do receive. Finally, the deductibility subsidy has been reduced, thereby bringing a closer correspondence between the amount a state or local government chooses to spend and the amount of revenue it must raise.

Some would argue that the changes in the 1980s do not represent a structural shift but rather only some temporary reactions to the times, and that such temporary breaks have long characterized the state and local government sector.[31] While it is true that the sector share of GNP and the ratio of taxes to personal income have increased during this decade, both are just now back to their pre–Proposition 13 levels. It also could be said that fiscal behavior in the 1980s has been a product of conservative politics and economics, and in time even this will change. Yet, the "turning point" in state and local government finances seems to have been reached about 10–12 years ago and this is a long period for a temporary change. Moreover, history suggests that once a new pattern of behavior is established by governments, it takes some form of shock to displace this behavior.[32]

Why has the U.S. fiscal system become more decentralized? The conventional reason for a push to stronger local government is the desire to get government decision making closer to the people. Centrally imposed expenditure mandates or direct central expenditures, unless they correct for some externality that local governments could not or would not take into account, impose a welfare loss on society because local budgets do not correspond with local preferences. Decentralization, it is argued, will lead to more citizen participation in government and to a greater degree of accountability of local government officials to their constituencies.

It was not these traditional arguments that led to fiscal decentralization in the U.S. in the 1980s. The impetus came more from the notion that a smaller federal sector and a less interventionist government sector would allow American business to perform better. The tax reforms of 1981 and 1986 reduced personal tax rates and the elasticity of the federal income tax and made it all but impossible to go back on the federal aid retrenchment program. Grant consolidation and deregulation were peas from the same policy pod, and the reduction of the tax expenditure for deductibility was a way to both reduce the deficit and place state and local governments on the same playing field as other competitors for the use of GNP.

In many ways the setting was just right for the shift to decentralization. The president was enormously popular and a reduced federal involvement in the economy was at the core of his program. The balance of payments deficit had popularized the ideas of flagging productivity, the declining competitiveness of American business, and the need for less government spending and more private investment. The federal income tax was seen by most as the chief culprit—complicated, unfair, and a disincentive to investors and entrepreneurs—and the move to a lower rate and a flatter rate structure with elimination of some tax expenditures was accepted as a fair trade.

State and local governments seemed to be in a relatively good position to take the hits of grant retrenchment and removal of part of the deductibility subsidy. They had accumulated a substantial surplus during the long expansion and would be able to draw this down to buffer the reduced federal subsidies, and state and local government taxes were not high by historical standards. Anyway, state and local governments had been getting by with less. A new fiscal conservatism had grown up in the aftermath of the 1975 recession and the tax limitation movement. Finally, regional shifts in economic activity had reduced the interstate disparity in income so that the equalization mandate of the federal grant system no longer seemed as important as it once had.

The result of this confluence of factors is that we live in a much more decentralized fiscal system now than we did ten years ago. A greater fraction of every dollar's worth of public services consumed is directly provided by subnational governments, and the gap between what a state or local government spends and the amount of revenue it must raise has narrowed. An increasing share of state and local government budgets is being financed by user and benefit charges, and other nontax revenues. As the longer term reaction to the provisions of the 1986 tax reform unfolds, and if federal grant reductions continue, it is possible that state and local government budgets will grow more slowly and that fiscal competition among the states will become more intense.

The 1980s has been a time of rethinking the objectives of government in the U.S. and sorting out the roles of the three levels of government. The general tenor has been a shift in emphasis from the redistribution of income to efficiency. The results of this have shown up in both an improved fiscal responsibility at all levels of government and a growing population of the poor. In this new setting, state and local governments have been given more responsibility to allocate resources—that function which they do best. The next step in the sorting out process is to assign a responsibility for redressing disparities among state and local governments and for determining a proper division of responsibilty for looking after the poor.

Notes

1. Anyone studying the United States federal system is in the debt of the Advisory Commission on Intergovernmental Relations (ACIR). In particular, their excellent biennial compilation *Significant Features of Fiscal Federalism* is invaluable in tracking the development of state and local government finances.

2. See Roy Bahl, *Financing State and Local Governments in the 1980s* (New York: Oxford University Press, 1984), chapter 2.

3. ACIR, *Significant Features of Fiscal Federalism*, 1980–81 edition, p. 29.

4. Reported by Robert Gleason "Federalism's Fiscal Shifts," *Intergovernmental Perspective* 14, 4 (Fall 1988), 26.

5. The term "social welfare expenditures" is used here to include all health, education, and welfare expenditures, and Social Security.

6. Richard P. Nathan and John R. Lago, "Intergovernmental Relations in the Reagan Era," *Public Budgeting and Finance* 8 (Autumn 1988), 15–29.

7. *Survey of Current Business*, April 1988, p. 13.

8. In Table 4.4, we define "average" as the unweighted mean value of the variable across the fifty states. For our purposes, this seems more appropriate than a weighted mean for defining a benchmark against which to compare interstate variations.

9. The measure of relative variation used in Table 4.4 is the coefficient of variation, i.e., the standard deviation as a percent of the mean. The smaller the coefficient, the less dispersed the distribution. For example, the reduction in the coefficient for the ratio of federal aid to personal income between 1967 and 1987 means that the states are grouped more closely about the mean in the later year.

10. ACIR, *1986 State Fiscal Capacity and Effort*, Information Report M–165 (Washington, DC: U.S. Government Printing Office, 1988).

11. Steven Gold and Judy Zelio, "Interstate Tax Comparisons and How They Have Changed Over Time," *Tax Notes* (March 20, 1989), pp. 1501–1512.

12. The New York case is reported in detail in Roy Bahl, "Federal Policy," in *Setting Municipal Priorities*, Raymond Horton and Charles Brecher, eds. (New York: New York University Press, 1988), chapter 2.

13. See, for example, Thomas E. Borcherding, and Robert T. Deacon, "The Demand for Services of Non Federal Governments," *American Economic Review* 62 (December 1972), pp. 891–901; and Roy Bahl, Marvin Johnson, and Michael Wasylenko, "State and Local Government Expenditure Determinants: The Traditional View and a New Approach," in *Public Employment and State and Local Government Finance*, Roy Bahl, Jesse Burkhead, and Bernard Jump, eds. (Cambridge, MA: Ballinger Publishing, 1980), chapter 4.

14. Only approximately $2 billion of this amount was paid by the states to the federal government, primarily to support the supplemental security income program which started in 1974.

15. This section updates parts of Roy Bahl and William Duncombe, "State and Local Government Finances: Was There a Structural Break in the Reagan Years," *Growth and Change* 19, 4 (Fall 1988), pp. 30–48.

16. The problems with interpreting the surplus measure are reviewed in Bahl, *Financing State and Local Governments*, chapter 2.

17. See Steven Gold, "Preparing for the Next Recession: Rainy Day Funds and Other Tools for States," National Conference of State Legislatures, Legislative Finance Paper #41, December 1983.

18. John Shannon, "Federal and State-Local Spenders Go Their Separate Ways," *American Intergovernmental Relations Today*, Robert J. Dilger, ed. (Englewood Cliffs, NJ: Prentice Hall, 1986), pp. 28–46.

19. Phillip Dearborn, "Fiscal Conditions in Large American Cities, 1971–84," paper prepared for the National Academy of Sciences, Committee on National Urban Policy, 1986, p. 36.

20. One estimate is that the relative tax price of the sales tax will increase by eight percent because of the reform. This is discussed in Dennis Zimmerman, "Federal Tax Reform and State Use of the Sales Tax," *Proceedings of the Seventy-Ninth Annual Meeting of the National Tax Association-Tax Institute of America*, pp. 325–33, November 1986.

21. Edward Gramlich, "The Deductibility of State and Local Taxes," *National Tax Journal* (December 1985), 447–464.

22. Daphne Kenyon, "Direct Estimates of the Effects of Tax Deductibility on State Tax Mix and the Level of State Taxing and Spending," mimeo, 1985.

23. Robert Inman, "Does Deductibility Influence Local Taxation," National Bureau of Economic Research (NBER) Working Paper 1714 (October 1985).

24. Martin Feldstein and Gilbert Metcalf, "The Effect of Federal Tax Deductibility on State and Local Taxes and Spending," *Journal of Political Economy* 95, 4 (August 1987), 710–736.

25. These effects are discussed in James R. Follain and Patrick H. Hendershott, *Tax Reform and Real Estate: The Impact of the Senate Finance Committee Plan* (Washington, DC: The Urban Institute, 1986).

26. Office of the State Comptroller, "The Potential Impact of Federal Tax Law Changes on New York City and New York State," mimeo, New York City, 1987.

27. There is a longstanding debate in the literature about whether fiscal incentives matter in the location choices of firms. The argument that they are not important is made in D.W. Carlton, "The Location and Employment Choices of New Firms: An Econometric Model with Discrete and Continuous Endogenous Variables," *Review of Economics and Statistics* 65, 1 (1983), 32–40. For the opposing view, and some empirical evidence, see Leslie Papke, "Subnational Taxation and Capital Mobility: Estimates of Tax-Price Elasticities," *National Tax Journal* 40, 2 (June 1987), 191–204.

28. Roy Bahl, "Industrial Policy and the States: How Will They Pay?" *Journal of the American Planning Association* (1986), reprinted in *The State and Local Industrial Policy Question*, Harvey A. Goldstein, ed. (Chicago, IL: Planners Press, American Planning Association, 1987).

29. John Kasarda, "Jobs, Migration, and Emerging Urban Mismatches," in *Urban Change and Poverty*, Michael McGeary and Laurence Lynn, eds., 148–97 (Washington, DC: National Academy Sciences Press, 1988).

30. William Julius Wilson, "The Urban Underclass in Advanced Industrial

Society," in *The New Urban Reality*, Paul E. Peterson, ed., 129–160 (Washington, DC: Brookings Institution, 1985).

31. See, for example, Deil S. Wright, *Understanding Intergovernmental Relations*, 3d edition (Pacific Grove, CA: Brooks/Cole Publishing, 1988), chapter 12.

32. This "displacement effect" is analyzed in Alan Peacock and Jack Wiseman, *The Growth of Public Expenditures in the United Kingdom* (London: Allen & Unwin, 1967).

State Finances in the New Era
of Fiscal Federalism

STEVEN D. GOLD

The 1980s have been a turbulent period for state governments. As the federal government wrestled with its gargantuan budget deficit, the states emerged as leaders in domestic policy. The states had to confront a series of problems—the legacy of the tax revolt of the late 1970s, cutbacks of federal aid, the most severe recession since the 1930s, a crisis of confidence in our educational system, federal tax reform, and a heightened level of intergovernmental competition.

With so many powerful forces affecting the states, it has been difficult to discern trends in the development of state fiscal policy. This chapter attempts to clear away the confusion, describing how state tax and spending policies have evolved and dispelling some of the misconceptions.

There are least six major sources of the confusion which can be found in the comments of journalists, scholars, and others. Most of this confusion results from the tendency to view developments in isolation.

- What may appear to be major policy changes may actually be attempts to restore the previous status quo. For example, a large tax cut in one year may be a reaction to a tax increase a few years earlier; likewise, a big spending increase may follow a previous period of fiscal austerity.
- Some discretionary actions have high visibility, while equally important changes may go virtually unnoticed. This can happen for several reasons: revenue may increase or decrease because of changes in the tax base rather than changes in tax rates, which are more noticeable; the costs of providing some services may increase unavoidably, so that baseline

Research for this paper was conducted as part of NCSL's Fiscal Federalism Project, which has been funded by a grant from the Ford Foundation. The views expressed are the author's and should not be attributed to NCSL or the Ford Foundation.

spending has to increase to maintain service levels; inflation may cause major changes in real relationships even though nominal changes are avoided; and government leaders may find it politically expedient to avoid calling attention to some of the mechanisms that are built into the system.

• Important changes in trends may not be observed if analysts use arbitrary years to begin and end their analyses. For example, the actions of state and local governments in the 1980s differ in some important respects from those in the 1970s, but this fact may be overlooked if the entire period from 1970 to 1987 is viewed as a unit.

• Local government developments need to be recognized along with state trends, but they should be considered separately. Often one of two analytical errors occurs: either state and local governments are lumped together, ignoring significant differences in their actions; or states are viewed by themselves, failing to take into account how their policies affect local governments.

• Important variations always exist among the fifty states, and if something occurs in a few high-visibility states (e.g., California, New York, and Massachusetts), there is a tendency to assume automatically that it is a general phenomenon, even though it may not be.[1]

• To understand the response of states to federal initiatives, one must view them in the context of the other forces influencing state policies. Often, for example, journalists have interpreted state tax increases as responses to federal aid cutbacks when other forces, such as the economy or efforts to improve schools, were more important.

While the main focus of this article is on state policies since 1978, in order to provide proper perspective it also traces some developments and examines some trends in local fiscal behavior back to 1970. It consists of six sections:

• Tax policy;
• Federal aid cutbacks;
• Fiscal conditions;
• Expenditure policy in general;
• Education spending; and
• Outlook for the next decade.

Tax Policy

States collect more than $270 billion per year in tax revenue.[2] This is more than twice as much as they raised as recently as 1979 and more than five times as much as they collected in 1970. While this seems like an enormous increase at first glance, its magnitude does not appear so tremendous when placed in perspective relative to the growth of the economy and local taxes.

Table 5.1 shows how state and local tax revenue has changed in relation to personal income over the period 1970 to 1987. One of the most remarkable facts shown by this table is that state-local taxes were just about the same proportion of personal income in 1970 as they were seventeen years later. This constancy masks some significant fluctuations that occurred during the intervening years. There was a big jump between 1970 and 1973, when the all-time peak of 12.41 percent of personal income was reached. This was followed by a decrease and then another rise that climaxed in 1977 and 1978.

The last month of fiscal year 1978 for most states was June.[3] On the sixth day of that month, California voters overwhelmingly approved Proposition 13, which cut their property taxes more than in half, thereby triggering a tax revolt that spread to many other states and the federal government. The round of tax reductions that then occurred was followed by two severe recessions in the early 1980s, causing a 13 percent drop in state-local tax revenue as a proportion of personal income by 1982. Because the fiscal position of most states was severely depressed, they responded in 1983 with a broad array of tax increases, which, along with the national economic recovery that began in November 1982, brought about a dramatic improvement in the health of state finances.[4]

The years 1984 and 1985 were dominated by the expiration, repeal, or rollback of many of the personal income tax increases enacted in late 1982 and 1983.[5] Because these tax cuts were offset by continued revenue growth resulting from inflation and the improvement of the economy, as well as tax increases in economically depressed energy states, tax revenue in 1985 and 1986 did not fall much as a proportion of personal income despite the well publicized tax cuts. Then in 1987 there was another jump in revenue, to a considerable extent resulting from the phase-in of federal tax reform, which temporarily boosted state tax collections.

The most important generalization from this capsule history is that state tax policy has been characterized by a series of reversals of direction. Decreases have followed increases and have been succeeded by further increases, leaving us not much different at the end from where we started. This absence of a net increase is itself a noteworthy develop-

Table 5.1

State and Local Tax Revenue per $100 of Personal Income, 1970 to 1987

Fiscal year	Total	Local	State	State				
				General sales	Personal income	Corporation income	Severance	Other
1987	$11.48	$4.48	$7.02	$2.26	$2.16	$0.59	$0.12	$1.89
1986	11.24	4.37	6.89	2.26	2.04	0.55	0.19	1.85
1985	11.28	4.34	6.97	2.25	2.06	0.57	0.23	1.86
1984	11.30	4.35	6.96	2.21	2.09	0.55	0.26	1.85
1983	10.68	4.25	6.46	2.02	1.88	0.50	0.28	1.78
1982	10.59	4.12	6.49	2.01	1.82	0.56	0.31	1.79
1981	10.85	4.20	6.67	2.07	1.82	0.63	0.28	1.87
1980	11.02	4.26	6.78	2.14	1.84	0.66	0.21	1.93
1979	11.37	4.46	6.94	2.19	1.81	0.67	0.16	2.11
1978	12.08	5.01	7.10	2.21	1.82	0.67	0.16	2.23
1977	12.15	5.17	7.02	2.14	1.77	0.64	0.15	2.32
1976	11.98	5.17	6.85	2.10	1.65	0.56	0.16	2.38
1975	11.74	5.09	6.68	2.07	1.57	0.55	0.15	2.34
1974	11.93	5.16	6.81	2.07	1.57	0.55	0.11	2.51
1973	12.41	5.43	7.01	2.04	1.60	0.56	0.09	2.72
1972	12.24	5.51	6.77	1.99	1.47	0.50	0.09	2.72
1971	11.50	5.26	6.27	1.88	1.24	0.42	0.09	2.64
1970	11.32	5.07	6.29	1.86	1.20	0.49	0.09	2.65

Sources: For tax revenue, U.S. Census Bureau, *Governmental Finances* (Washington, DC: U.S. Government Printing Office, various years); U.S. Census Bureau, *State Government Finances* (Washington, DC: U.S. Government Printing Office, various years). For personal income, U.S. Department of Commerce, *Survey of Current Business* 67 (August 1987), 44.

Notes: Revenue for each fiscal year is divided by personal income in the calendar year that ended during it. District of Columbia taxes are included with those for local governments. Calculations involving state taxes exclude personal income in the District of Columbia.

ment, since it marks a reversal of the trend earlier in the postwar period, when state and local taxes tended to rise much faster than personal income. For example, between 1950 and 1970, they rose from 7.71 percent of personal income to 11.32 percent.

There are several reasons for the halt in the trend toward rising tax burdens. The most important demographic change occurred in 1973 when enrollment in elementary and secondary schools peaked. The cost of educating the baby boomers was one of the main forces that had caused taxes to increase in the 1950s and 1960s, and when that phase ended it eliminated a major source of pressure for higher taxes. The poorer performance of the national economy also contributed to the slowdown of tax increases. After 1973, economic growth was much slower than it had been in the previous quarter century, and taxpayers were more resistant to paying higher taxes when their real income was stagnant or declining than they had been when the standard of living was rising strongly.[6] A general trend toward fiscal conservatism at all levels of government, and increased intergovernmental competition were two more factors that slowed the upward momentum of taxes.

A significant shift in relative state and local tax levels has also occurred. Although state taxes are considerably higher than they were in 1970, local taxes are much lower. This happened because states took many steps to reduce local reliance on property taxes, which are the major source of local tax revenue.[7] (The property tax accounted for 84.9 percent of local tax revenue in 1970 and 73.7 percent in 1987.)

The increased relative reliance on state taxation occurred during the 1970s. In the 1980s, by contrast, local taxes have kept pace with the rise in state taxes. The proportion of state-local taxes raised by local governments fell from 44.8 percent in 1970 to 38.7 percent in 1980 and increased to 39 percent in 1987. The halt in the relative increase of state taxes has occurred because the fiscal condition of the states has not been as strong in this decade as it was in the 1970s. This really has been, in the words of John Shannon, former executive director of the U.S. Advisory Commission on Intergovernmental Relations (ACIR), an era of ''fend-for-yourself federalism.''

It is important to recognize, however, that both state and local taxes have risen in the 1980s relative to federal taxes. In 1987 states accounted for 26.1 percent of total tax revenue raised by all levels of government (not counting taxes for trust funds like Social Security). This represents a considerable increase from 20.6 percent in 1970 and 23.9 percent in 1980.[8]

As Table 5.1 demonstrates, the structure of state tax systems has changed considerably since 1970. The most important change is the ever greater role of the personal income tax, which has grown from 19.1 percent of state tax revenue in 1970 to 30.8 percent in 1987. An important reason for the increase in the 1980s has been the relatively high elasticity of this tax; that is, its revenue tends to grow faster than personal income because inflation and economic growth push taxpayers into higher tax brackets over time and because personal exemptions and standard deductions are generally not indexed to inflation, reducing the proportion of income they protect from taxation.

The general sales tax has also increased relative to personal income, although not as rapidly as the income tax. This increase has occurred because tax rates have been raised, more than offsetting the erosion of the tax base. The tax base narrowed for two reasons: new exemptions granted by states and the increased proportion of spending on services, which are taxed relatively lightly compared to goods.[9]

Together, the general sales and personal income taxes account for 63 percent of state tax revenue. When states need substantial infusions of revenue, these taxes are the prime sources from which they can be obtained.

Revenue from the state corporation income tax has lagged far behind the growth of the personal income tax. As in the case of the sales tax, states have been increasing their nominal tax rates to offset the relatively slow growth of the tax base. Because of these tax rate increases, state corporation income tax revenue has grown relative to federal corporation income tax revenue. Between 1970 and 1987 the proportion of corporation income taxes paid to states rose from 10.2 percent to 19.4 percent.[10]

Because most states tie their personal and corporation income taxes to the federal definition of income in some manner, these taxes could have been strongly affected by federal tax reform, which broadened the tax base, especially for corporations. Any permanent effects of federal tax reform, however, are not reflected in Table 5.1 because that table extends only through fiscal year 1987. Most of the potential personal income tax ''windfall'' that states might have received was avoided by tax changes enacted in 1987 sessions, but most states did not act to offset a corporate ''windfall.'' Whether a corporate ''windfall'' actually develops remains to be seen; as of early 1989 there was no sign of one.[11]

Federal tax reform did affect fiscal 1987 tax collections in a temporary fashion. Many investors realized capital gains in the last few months of

Table 5.2

State-Local Tax Revenue per $100 of Personal Income, Fiscal Years 1970, 1978, and 1987

State	FY1970		FY1978		Change	FY1987
	Level	Rank	Level	Rank		Rank
New England						
Connecticut	$10.22	35	$11.02	32	$11.38	23
Maine	12.17	15	12.33	13	12.77	6
Massachusetts	11.82	17	14.46	5	11.93	13
New Hampshire	9.09	49	9.71	48	8.99	50
Rhode Island	10.93	29	12.00	17	11.93	13
Vermont	14.22	2	13.46	9	12.38	9
Middle Atlantic						
Delaware	10.43	33	11.94	18	11.88	15
Maryland	11.77	18	12.31	14	11.47	20
New Jersey	10.05	36	11.87	20	11.35	24
New York	14.37	1	16.30	1	16.25	3
Pennsylvania	10.65	31	11.61	26	10.95	28
Great Lakes						
Illinois	11.30	23	10.90	34	10.62	32
Indiana	9.80	40	9.87	44	9.98	42
Michigan	11.35	22	12.23	15	12.09	11
Ohio	8.92	50	9.52	49	10.87	29
Wisconsin	13.97	3	13.58	7	12.53	7
Plains						
Iowa	12.22	14	10.98	33	11.40	22
Kansas	11.28	24	11.12	30	10.36	37
Minnesota	11.99	16	13.56	8	12.80	5
Missouri	9.79	41	9.46	50	9.11	49
Nebraska	11.27	25	11.79	21	10.60	34
North Dakota	12.49	10	11.56	27	10.12	40
South Dakota	13.47	4	11.10	31	10.12	41

Southeast						
Alabama	9.51	47	9.80	45	9.67	46
Arkansas	9.73	44	9.80	46	9.42	48
Florida	9.85	39	9.79	47	9.60	47
Georgia	9.99	37	10.66	39	10.40	36
Kentucky	10.29	34	10.82	36	10.77	31
Louisiana	11.60	21	11.70	25	10.86	30
Mississippi	12.48	11	11.13	29	10.19	39
North Carolina	10.45	32	10.65	40	11.10	25
South Carolina	9.94	38	10.80	37	11.07	26
Tennessee	9.58	45	10.21	42	9.74	45
Virginia	9.73	43	10.69	38	10.25	38
West Virginia	10.88	30	11.16	28	11.51	18
Southwest						
Arizona	12.63	6	13.66	6	12.07	12
New Mexico	12.50	9	12.65	12	11.61	17
Oklahoma	9.74	42	10.22	41	9.82	44
Texas	9.53	46	10.02	43	9.92	43
Rocky Mountain						
Colorado	11.62	20	11.70	24	10.61	33
Idaho	10.96	28	10.85	35	10.45	35
Montana	12.41	13	12.95	11	11.44	21
Utah	12.52	8	11.91	19	12.49	8
Wyoming	12.42	12	15.28	3	17.33	2
Far West						
Alaska	9.17	48	16.04	2	17.48	1
California	12.62	7	14.62	4	11.68	16
Hawaii	13.45	5	13.17	10	13.39	4
Nevada	11.75	19	11.73	23	10.98	27
Oregon	11.11	26	11.78	22	12.21	10
Washington	11.11	27	12.02	16	11.50	19
U.S. Average	$11.33		$12.08		$11.46	

Sources: U.S. Census Bureau, *Government Finances in 1987;* U.S. Census Bureau, *State Government Finances in 1987* (Washington, DC: U.S. Government Printing Office); U.S. Commerce Department, *Survey of Current Business* (August 1987).

1986 because the maximum tax rate on such gains was scheduled to increase from 20 percent to 28 percent. Corporations also had an incentive to accelerate their state tax payments in 1986 so that they could be deducted before federal tax rates decreased. For these reasons the 1987 revenue from both income taxes shown in Table 5.1 was inflated. Many states experienced unusually low revenue increases in the following year because the temporary effects of federal reform were no longer present. The well publicized 1988 revenue shortfalls in California, Massachusetts, and New York are to a considerable extent a result of this phenomenon.

Table 5.1 also shows that severance tax revenue was extremely volatile, more than tripling as a proportion of personal income between 1970 and 1982 and then falling almost back to the 1970 level. The fluctuations reflect the rise and fall of energy prices over this period. Severance taxes, mostly from the production of oil and natural gas, are important revenue sources in eight states,[12] and the fiscal condition of those states deviated substantially from national trends: they did not suffer as most other states did in the early 1980s, but they were much more depressed in the mid- and late 1980s.

The final column of Table 5.1 reflects all other state taxes, particularly excise taxes on such products as gasoline, tobacco, alcoholic beverages, utilities, and insurance. Revenue from these taxes has usually tended to fall relative to other state taxes because (a) many of them are based on quantities sold rather than the value of sales (and therefore do not automatically increase with inflation), and (b) demand for many of these products tends to grow relatively slowly. In the 1980s, however, revenue from these miscellaneous taxes did actually keep up with the growth of personal income. This occurred because states were not as reluctant as in the past to raise gasoline and cigarette taxes and also because revenue from utility and insurance taxes (which are typically based on sales rather than units) increased substantially.

The aggregate trends that have been discussed above naturally obscure a wide variety of experiences in particular states. Table 5.2 shows how the ratio of state-local tax revenue to personal income changed between 1970, 1978, and 1987. In general, increases predominated between 1970 and 1978, and the changes were relatively small from 1978 to 1987.[13]

The two states with the largest percentage decreases in tax levels after 1978 were California and Massachusetts, the states where major tax revolt initiatives passed (Proposition 13 in 1978 and Proposition 2½ in

1980). Except in these states and Idaho,[14] voters consistently have rejected proposals that would result in major tax reductions. Many other states enacted tax limitations, either through initiatives, referenda, or legislation. These limitations usually restricted the growth of revenue to the increase of personal income. Voters have shown the ability to distinguish between radical measures that would seriously interfere with service provision and moderate measures that merely keep taxes from rising faster than the growth of the economy.[15]

Although this discussion has focused on tax revenue, one should recognize that governments also can obtain money from other sources. As Table 5.3 shows, states have come to depend increasingly on nontax revenue in the past two decades. There is an important distinction between the two main components to this nontax revenue. *Charges* have risen moderately faster than personal income, growing from 0.8 percent of personal income in 1970 to 0.91 percent in 1987. *Miscellaneous revenue* has grown much more rapidly, soaring from 0.45 percent of personal income to 1.09 percent. Most miscellaneous revenue is not a burden on citizens in the same sense that taxes are. Interest payments account for about half of miscellaneous revenue, and their growth has been in part a result of higher market interest rates and improved cash management practices. Royalties also have been a major source of increased revenue for those states fortunate to have major oil and natural gas reserves.[16]

This review of how state revenue systems have evolved has concentrated on quantitative trends, but the qualitative dimension of taxes also needs to be recognized. States did a great deal in the late 1950s, 1960s, and early 1970s, to strengthen their tax systems, particularly by enacting sales and income taxes where they were previously absent. The significant tax reforms of those years laid the groundwork for the growth of state government in the following period.

The economic problems of the early 1980s led many states to create tax study commissions to review their tax policies. These commissions helped to pave the way for the wave of state income tax reform that was sparked in 1987 by federal tax reform. Most states seized the opportunity afforded by federal reform to restructure their income taxes, particularly by increasing personal exemptions and standard deductions, reducing tax rates when they were above average, simplifying provisions, and providing tax relief for the poor.[17]

Some commentators on state policies have been led astray by either

Table 5.3

State General Revenue per $100 of Personal Income, 1970, 1978, and 1987

Category of revenue	1970	1978	1987
Total	$10.19	$11.85	$11.93
Federal aid	2.52	3.14	2.71
Taxes	6.29	7.10	7.02
Charges	0.80	0.85	0.91
Higher education	0.46	0.47	0.51
Miscellaneous	0.45	0.55	1.09
Interest	0.19	0.28	0.54

Sources: U.S. Census Bureau, *State Government Finances in* (various years) (Washington, DC: U.S. Government Printing Office); U.S. Department of Commerce, *Survey of Current Business* 67 (August 1987), 44.

Note: Revenue received by states from local governments is not shown in the table. It was $0.13 in 1970, $0.20 in 1978, and $0.20 in 1987.

of two pitfalls, concentrating on trends during a single year or two, or arbitrarily comparing changes between two years. For example, if you compare state-local tax revenue in 1987 with its level in 1980, it rose faster than personal income, but if you compare it with 1978, it rose slower. Since there is no absolutely correct comparison, the best approach is to consider information for all years in the period under analysis.

Federal Aid Cutbacks

One of the most dramatic developments affecting state and local finances in the 1980s is the cutback of federal aid, which was a theme of President Reagan's budgets. To a considerable extent, however, the perception is not wholly consistent with the reality. Table 5.4 shows how much federal aid state and local governments received each year from 1970 to 1987. As it indicates, the only annual decrease occurred in 1982, when a 3.7 percent reduction was reported.[18]

There is a dramatic difference between the paths of federal aid to state and local governments. Aid to localities increased much more rapidly in the 1970s and fared much more poorly once the era of federal retrenchment began. Federal aid to local governments was 8.6 times as great in

Table 5.4

Federal Aid to State and Local Governments, 1970 to 1987 (millions of dollars)

Year	Total	State	Local
1987	$114,996	$95,463	$19,533
1986	113,099	92,666	20,433
1985	106,193	84,469	21,724
1984	97,052	76,140	20,912
1983	89,983	68,962	21,021
1982	86,945	66,026	20,919
1981	90,294	67,868	22,427
1980	83,029	61,892	21,136
1979	75,164	54,548	20,616
1978	69,592	50,200	19,393
1977	62,575	45,938	16,637
1976	55,589	42,013	13,576
1975	47,054	36,148	10,906
1974	41,831	31,632	10,199
1973	39,256	31,353	7,903
1972	31,253	26,791	4,462
1971	26,146	22,754	3,391
1970	21,857	19,252	2,605

Source: U.S. Census Bureau, *Governmental Finances in* (year) (Washington, DC: U.S. Government Printing Office).

1981, its peak year, as it had been in 1970. Aid to state governments in 1981 was "only" 3.5 times as much as it had been in 1970. After 1981 aid to states continued to grow, except for a reduction in 1982. By 1987, federal aid to states was 40 percent higher than it had been in 1981, but federal aid to local governments was 13 percent lower than in 1981. An important reason for the different paths of aid to states and localities is that the programs that were most vulnerable to federal cutbacks in the Reagan era were the relatively young programs begun during the Johnson and Nixon administrations. Many of these programs had broken precedent by giving aid directly to localities rather than using states as conduits, reflecting a widespread distrust of the states and doubt that they would administer programs in line with federal intent.

Federal aid to states fared better than federal aid to localities for two reasons. As discussed below, nearly half of federal aid to states is for means-tested entitlements. Although Aid to Families with Dependent Children (AFDC), Medicaid, and other programs for the poor were trimmed by the Omnibus Budget Reconciliation Act of 1981 (OBRA), Medicaid costs grew substantially in the 1980s, because the number of eligible persons grew, some services were added, and especially because the costs of providing medical care rose unavoidably at a high rate. States also benefited from increased highway spending. Secondly, some programs that formerly provided aid directly to localities were consolidated into block grants administered by states. While most of the money in these programs still reaches local governments, it is reported first as federal aid to states and later as state aid to localities. The block grants reflected both dissatisfaction with the confusing and cumbersome array of categorical programs and greater confidence that the states could competently and fairly administer the programs.[19]

Table 5.5 provides a different perspective by relating federal aid to personal income, which can be viewed as a proxy for the growth of the economy. It shows that 1978 was the peak year for federal aid, when it reached $4.34 per $100 of personal income. This reflects the fact that it was President Carter, not President Reagan, who started the process of halting the dynamic growth of federal aid. By 1987, federal aid was down 25 percent in relation to personal income, at $3.26 per $100.

Figure 5.1 shows the indexed changes in aid relative to personal income. Once again there is a dramatic difference between the patterns for state and local governments. Federal aid to states in 1987 was only 16 percent less than its 1976 high point, but aid to local governments was 55 percent less than its 1978 peak.

The composition of federal aid to states has changed considerably, as Table 5.6 shows. The largest component of aid in 1987 was Medicaid, accounting for 28 percent of the total, a much bigger proportion than its 20 percent in 1970. Other welfare spending rose dramatically in the early 1970s and has been on a downward trend since 1976. Highway spending has been a big loser, declining from 23 percent to 14 percent of total aid; it rebounded in 1984 and 1985 after the federal gasoline tax was increased but fell off again in 1987. Aid for health and hospitals trended upward from 1970 to 1977 but has been a constant proportion of personal income since then. Education aid is another loser. In the early 1970s it was the largest category of aid, but it has declined relative both to personal income and to total aid. In percentage terms, it suffered a larger decrease during the Reagan years than any other specific major aid category.

Table 5.5

Federal Aid to State and Local Governments per $100 of Personal Income, 1970 to 1987

Year	Total	State	Local
1987	$3.26	$2.70	$0.55
1986	3.41	2.79	0.62
1985	3.42	2.72	0.70
1984	3.42	2.69	0.74
1983	3.38	2.59	0.79
1982	3.46	2.63	0.83
1981	4.00	3.01	0.99
1980	4.09	3.05	1.04
1979	4.16	3.02	1.14
1978	4.34	3.13	1.21
1977	4.32	3.17	1.15
1976	4.25	3.21	1.04
1975	3.91	3.00	0.91
1974	3.82	2.89	0.93
1973	4.02	3.21	0.81
1972	3.52	3.02	0.50
1971	3.17	2.76	0.41
1970	2.85	2.51	0.34

Sources: Federal aid: U.S. Census Bureau, *Governmental Finances in* (year) (Washington, DC: U.S. Government Printing Office); personal income: U.S. Department of Commerce, *Survey of Current Business* (August 1987).

"Other" aid—programs that do not fall into one of the five major categories—also has experienced a big reduction. This miscellaneous category includes general purpose aid like General Revenue Sharing and categorical programs in areas such as housing and community development, transit, natural resources, and employment security administration. Its greatest loss was in the Carter years, with a big decrease between 1978 and 1981. After another big drop in 1982, miscellaneous aid has rebounded and actually was the fastest growing aid category between 1982 and 1987. The Carter decrease involved the end of the economic stimulus package of antirecession aid, and the state share of General Revenue Sharing, and the subsequent increase in part reflects the Reagan block grant approach.

Cutbacks in federal programs usually have their major impact on the people who benefit from the programs, not on the state and local

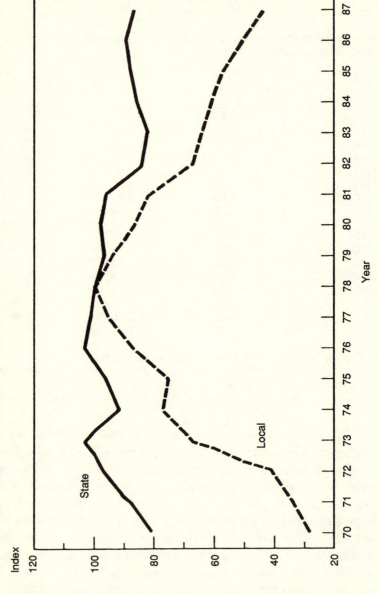

Figure 5.1. Federal Aid to State and Local Governments per $100 of Personal Income, 1970–1987 (1978 = 100)

Table 5.6

Federal Aid to States per $100 of Personal Income, 1970 to 1987

Year	Total	Education	Medicaid	Other welfare[a]	Health and hospitals	Highways	Other
1987	$2.71	$0.48	$0.76	$0.52	$0.11	$0.37	$0.48
1986	2.80	0.50	0.74	0.53	0.11	0.42	0.51
1985	2.73	0.50	0.71	0.54	0.11	0.41	0.46
1984	2.70	0.49	0.70	0.55	0.11	0.37	0.46
1983	2.60	0.50	0.70	0.54	0.11	0.34	0.42
1982	2.64	0.52	0.69	0.57	0.10	0.33	0.42
1981	3.02	0.63	0.72	0.57	0.12	0.42	0.58
1980	3.06	0.63	0.67	0.55	0.11	0.44	0.66
1979	3.03	0.60	0.67	0.57	0.11	0.39	0.70
1978	3.14	0.62	0.66	0.60	0.11	0.39	0.77
1977	3.19	0.63	0.67	0.63	0.11	0.44	0.71
1976	3.23	0.66	0.66	0.64	0.09	0.48	0.69
1975	3.01	0.66	0.57	0.62	0.09	0.44	0.64
1974	2.90	0.62	0.67	0.55	0.07	0.41	0.58
1973	3.23	0.66	0.62	0.79	0.06	0.48	0.62
1972	3.03	0.68	0.68	0.71	0.07	0.55	0.34
1971	2.77	0.67	0.55	0.62	0.06	0.59	0.29
1970	2.52	0.60	0.50	0.52	0.07	0.58	0.25

Sources: See Appendix.

Notes: Data are derived from various sources, which may not be entirely consistent. Federal aid has not been subtracted from corrections spending, but aid for corrections is a relatively small amount.

[a]Other welfare includes cash assistance payments and other support of and assistance to needy persons contingent upon their need.

governments that directly lose funding, unless they offset the federal cutbacks with their own revenue. In fact, some of the federal cuts enacted in 1981 actually eased state-local budget pressures in the short run by reducing eligibility for AFDC and Medicaid. In these cases and several others, it was the working poor who were the big losers from the federal cutbacks of the early 1980s.[20]

The impact of federal aid reductions on the states is discussed in a later section of this article on state spending. As reported there, field research by Richard Nathan and his associates and by the Urban Institute indicate that states replaced a significant amount of federal cutbacks with their own funds.

To assess the impact of federal aid cuts it is necessary to understand the effect of that aid on spending in the first place. To a limited extent, the aid is fungible. When fungible aid is reduced, the state government suffers a loss even if it does not appear to replace the aid with its own resources. The question is: How much fungibility was there in the programs that existed before the federal government cut back? If a program was for some purpose that the recipient would not have spent any money on if the program had not existed, the funds were not fungible except to the extent that there was reimbursement for indirect costs.[21]

Since General Revenue Sharing was the only type of federal aid that could be used for any purpose chosen by the recipient, its elimination directly hurt state budgets. States lost their own-third of this program's $7 billion in 1980, and cities and counties lost the remainder in 1986. The size of this program was, however, relatively small in comparison with total state and local budgets.[22]

It is difficult to trace the long run effect of federal aid reductions because state and local governments may respond to them in subtle ways that develop gradually over time. For example, when millions of the working poor lost Medicaid eligibility, they did not cease needing medical care, nor did some other nongovernmental program miraculously come to their aid. Many of them turned to state and local hospitals, which therefore required additional funding. *Eventually* states and localities responded indirectly to these federal aid cuts by increasing health spending, even if they did not directly replace the lost funds. Another way of making this general point is to observe that state and local governments may develop new approaches to respond to the same need as the federal program, but they may do it in a different way, one that is tailored to their local situation. Because of the diversity of responses, national generalizations are difficult if not impossible to make, with the information currently available at the national level.

Table 5.2 demonstrates that between 1978 and 1987 total state revenue rose from $11.85 to $11.93 per $100 of personal income despite a decrease in federal aid from $3.14 to $2.71 per $100 of personal income. In other words, revenue from other sources made up for the federal aid reductions. Does this mean that states raised taxes to offset the federal aid cuts?[23] Such a conclusion would be surprising, since no states explicitly raised taxes for that reason. In fact, state tax revenue fell slightly relative to personal income during this period, and it was miscellaneous revenue, especially from interest earnings, that rose sharply. A significant portion of this increase in miscellaneous revenue was not available for general state operations.[24]

Fiscal Conditions

State fiscal conditions are both a determinant and a result of state fiscal policies. When states are fiscally healthy, they can increase spending and/or cut taxes. When they are fiscally depressed, their range of options is restricted.

The other side of the coin, however, is that while state fiscal conditions are in part determined by fiscal policies, there are strong outside forces that also play a major role in determining the fiscal health of the states. The most important outside force affecting state fiscal conditions is the performance of state economies, which tend to vary in line with national economic trends. States are always hit hard by recessions, primarily because recessions depress tax collections and secondarily because they increase the demand for certain services, such as welfare. State tax systems are more vulnerable to a recession now than they were in the past because of the changes that have taken place in tax structures. The personal and corporate income tax and the sales tax are all sensitive to economic fluctuations. The sensitivity of the sales tax has increased because of the trend toward exempting food and drugs from the tax base. By exempting these necessities, states have made durable goods account for a larger proportion of tax revenue, and demand for durables is much more cyclical than the demand for nondurables.[25]

Other environmental factors that have influenced state fiscal conditions are the tax revolt and the increased level of intergovernmental fiscal competition. Both of these developments have inhibited the ability of states

Table 5.7

State General Fund and Rainy Day Fund Balances, 1978 to 1988

Year	Amount (billions of $)	Percentage of expenditures
1988	$9.8	4.2%
1987	6.7	3.1
1986	7.2	3.5
1985	9.7	5.2
1984	6.4	3.8
1983	2.3	1.5
1982	4.5	2.9
1981	6.5	4.4
1980	11.8	9.0
1979	11.2	8.7
1978	8.9	8.6

Source: National Governors' Association (NGA) and National Association of State Budget Officers (NASBO), *Fiscal Survey of the States: March 1989*, p.18.

Notes: No Rainy Day Funds are included prior to 1983, although some small balances were held in those funds. Figures for Rainy Day Funds are: 1988, $3.0 billion; 1987, $2.0 billion; 1986, $1.5 billion; 1985, $1.7 billion; 1984, $0.9 billion; and 1983, $0.3 billion.

to raise taxes, although they certainly have not prevented all tax increases. With only a few exceptions, major tax increases in the 1980s have occurred only when states were experiencing serious fiscal difficulties caused by unfavorable economic trends. Very few major tax increases have been sold as a means of improving service levels, and those exceptions were primarily for education in states where poor schools were perceived as a major impediment to economic development prospects.

Intergovernmental competition to attract and retain industry has been intense in part because of the severity of the 1980–82 recessions and the increased vulnerability of the economy to competition from overseas. The decrease in federal marginal tax rates also has exacerbated competition because it has substantially increased the burden of paying state and local taxes. In 1980, it cost a typical high income person only 30 cents to pay a dollar of tax to a state government because the federal tax rate was 70 percent. Now it costs that same person 72 cents to pay that dollar of state tax because the federal tax rate is only 28 percent. (Some high income taxpayers have an even higher tax rate—33 percent—so a dollar paid to a state costs only 67 cents.)

Intergovernmental competition has led to a reduction in marginal tax rates in states with above-average rates. It has also fostered the trend toward business tax incentives, either in the form of tax credits or exemptions for inventories from the property tax and manufacturing equipment from the sales tax. These policies have reduced the growth of state revenue.[26]

One of the best barometers of state fiscal conditions is the balances held in state general funds and budget stabilization funds. Those balances have been considerably lower in the 1980s than they were in the late 1970s. As Table 5.7 shows, in 1979 and 1980 states had between $11 billion and $12 billion in year-end balances, representing close to 9 percent of their annual general fund spending. Those balances plummeted in the early 1980s, falling to just $2.3 billion at the end of fiscal year 1983. Although they rebounded thereafter, they remained at much lower levels than in the 1970s, only in 1985 attaining the 5 percent level viewed by many experts as the prudent minimum to hold in reserve. An important reason why balances did not reach previous levels is the perception that the substantial balances in the 1970s contributed to the tax revolt. High balances tend to create the impression that taxes can be cut without sacrificing services; while that is true in the short run, it is not true once the reserves are exhausted. The widespread cuts in personal income taxes in 1984 and 1985 prevented states from accumulating balances of the magnitude they had held five years earlier.[27]

The increased prevalence of budget stabilization funds in the 1980s has created the impression that states are holding extra funds in reserve as a hedge against an economic downturn. This view is mistaken because to a considerable extent these stabilization funds have substituted for rather than supplemented the funds that states would have normally held. Close to two-thirds of the states now have such funds, but in most cases their size is relatively insignificant.[28] Most states are highly vulnerable to an economic slowdown.

Expenditure Policy

Some significant changes have occurred in the pattern of state spending, as Table 5.8 shows. The table shows state spending from the states' own resources, excluding federal aid.[29] The general pattern of state spending per $100 over the years since 1976 is similar to that for tax revenue shown in Table 5.1—a downtrend through 1983 followed by an upswing as the

Table 5.8

State Spending per $100 of Personal Income, Excluding Federal Aid, 1976 to 1987

Year	Total[a]	Higher education[b]	Elem.-sec. education[c]	Medicaid[d]	Other welfare[e]	Hospitals	Highways	Corrections	Other
1987	$8.77	$0.92	$2.28	$0.58	$0.37	$0.80	$0.72	$0.33	$2.77
1986	8.58	0.93	2.27	0.55	0.38	0.80	0.69	0.33	2.63
1985	8.44	0.92	2.23	0.56	0.37	0.78	0.66	0.30	2.62
1984	8.26	0.90	2.17	0.57	0.40	0.77	0.65	0.27	2.53
1983	8.14	0.90	2.16	0.56	0.37	0.79	0.66	0.25	2.45
1982	8.12	0.91	2.17	0.49	0.46	0.79	0.67	0.24	2.39
1981	8.27	0.93	2.28	0.48	0.52	0.80	0.71	0.23	2.32
1980	8.23	0.94	2.36	0.46	0.51	0.77	0.80	0.22	2.17
1979	8.11	0.94	2.30	0.42	0.50	0.75	0.79	0.21	2.20
1978	8.12	0.97	2.27	0.38	0.61	0.76	0.77	0.21	2.15
1977	8.33	0.96	2.28	0.38	0.60	0.77	0.77	0.20	2.37
1976	8.57	0.97	2.35	0.35	0.67	0.76	0.91	0.19	2.37

Sources: U.S. Census Bureau, *Government Finances in* (various years) (Washington, DC: U.S. Government Printing Office), Table 2; for higher education appropriations, data reported by Illionois State University, *The Grapevine,* as reproduced in John R. Wittstruck and Stephen M. Bragg, *Focus on Price* (Denver: State Higher Education Executive Officers, 1988), 1987–88 and previous issues. Medicaid spending is from Congressional Research Service, *Medicaid SourceBook: Background Data and Analysis* (November 1988), supplemented for census bureau reports on city and county finances and unpublished information provided by the Health Care Financing Administration. Personal income is from U.S. Commerce Department, *Survey of Current Business* (August 1987).

Notes: Data are derived from various sources, which may not be entirely consistent. Federal aid has not been subtracted from corrections spending, but aid for corrections is a relatively small amount.

[a]Total spending is what the U.S. Census Bureau labels general spending excluding federal aid. General spending includes all expenditures except for utilities, liquor stores, employee retirement, and other insurance trust programs. Spending for a fiscal year is divided by personal income for the calendar year that ends during it, e.g., fiscal year 1987 spending is divided by personal income in calendar year 1986. Personal income excludes income from the District of Columbia because it is considered a local government by the census bureau. (An exception is for elementary-secondary education spending, which does include the District of Columbia.)

[b]Higher education spending includes only appropriations, not spending financed by tuition or other fee revenue.

[c]Elementary-secondary education is state revenue provided to K–12 schools. It includes not only state financial aid but also state contributions for teacher retirement systems.

[d]Medicaid spending includes not only direct spending on state operated programs but also payments to local governments where they have partial responsibility for funding Medicaid. Locally-funded expenditures are not included.

[e]Other welfare includes cash assistance payments and other support of and assistance to needy persons contingent upon their need.

Table 5.9

State-Local Spending per $100 of Personal Income for Aid to Families with Dependent Children (AFDC) and Supplemental Security Income (SSI), 1970 to 1987

Year	AFDC	SSI
1987	$0.24	$0.08
1986	0.25	0.08
1985	0.25	0.07
1984	0.26	0.07
1983	0.27	0.08
1982	0.27	0.08
1981	0.29	0.09
1980	0.30	0.10
1979	0.31	0.10
1978	0.34	0.10
1977	0.36	0.11
1976	0.38	0.12
1975	0.36	0.12
1974	0.34	0.13
1973	0.35	0.15
1972	0.36	N/A
1971	0.33	N/A
1970	0.21	N/A

Source: U.S. Committee on Ways and Means, House of Representatives, *Background Material and Data on Programs Within the Jurisdiction of the Committee on Ways and Means*, 1988 Edition (March 24, 1988), pp. 425, 527.

Notes: These figures include spending financed by local governments but not by federal aid. 1987 figures are estimated. SSI spending in 1973 refers to predecessor programs (old-age assistance, and aid to the blind and permanently and totally disabled). AFDC spending includes administrative costs as well as benefits. Information has been converted from federal fiscal years and calendar years to state fiscal years.

economy improved and taxes were raised. Spending is, however, less volatile than tax revenue, so the peaks and valleys are not as pronounced. As in the case of tax revenue, the 1987 level of spending relative to personal income was not much different from what it was in the late 1970s. In other words, spending tended to increase in proportion to personal income.

Education takes the largest part of state budgets, accounting for more than 36 percent of total outlays, counting both elementary-secondary and higher education. As Table 5.8 shows, spending for both types of

Table 5.10

State Spending for Health and Hospitals per $100 of Personal Income, 1970 to 1987

Year	Health	Hospitals
1987	$0.40	$0.51
1986	0.39	0.52
1985	0.38	0.52
1984	0.34	0.54
1983	0.34	0.56
1982	0.33	0.56
1981	0.35	0.57
1980	0.32	0.56
1979	0.29	0.57
1978	0.28	0.59
1977	0.27	0.61
1976	0.25	0.60
1975	0.26	0.59
1974	0.20	0.57
1973	0.19	0.56
1972	0.22	0.57
1971	0.18	0.57
1970	0.16	0.55

Sources: U.S. Census Bureau, *Governmental Finances in* (year) (Washington, DC: U.S. Government Printing Office); personal income: U.S. Department of Commerce, *Survey of Current Business* (August 1987).
Note: These figures include spending financed by federal aid.

education programs has been relatively steady as a proportion of personal income in the period since 1976. Spending for both was slightly lower per dollar of personal income in 1987 than 11 years earlier but a little higher than in 1983. The relatively small increase between 1983 and 1987 is somewhat surprising in view of the national spotlight that fell on education during this period and the high level of activity in the education arena. The next section of this chapter takes a more detailed look at fiscal trends in education.

The two fastest growing parts of the budget are Medicaid and corrections. All other categories of spending have been hurt by competition from these two areas. Corrections spending has increased for several reasons, two of the most important being that (1) tougher sentencing policies have led to tremendous increases in prisoner populations and (2) courts have mandated that overcrowding be relieved and conditions generally improved.[30] Although corrections grew most rapidly (more than 70 percent faster than personal income), it is such a small proportion of the budget that Medicaid increases have been more significant in absolute terms. The cost of Medicaid—health services for the poor—has been driven higher by the rapid escalation in the price of medical services as well as by increases in coverage and eligible services mandated by the federal government.[31]

The biggest loser in the competition for state dollars has been welfare spending other than Medicaid, which includes Aid to Families with Dependent Children (AFDC), general assistance payments to persons not covered by the federally-mandated categorical programs, and other services to the poor. Unlike most other parts of the budget that tend to increase automatically simply because of higher salaries for employees, benefits per recipient from these programs (which are determined by states) have lagged far behind inflation. In the twelve years from 1975 to 1987, the real value of AFDC benefits for a family of four persons in the median state fell 24 percent.[32] In addition, a smaller proportion of the poor are eligible for AFDC than in the past, because of changes instituted by the federal government in 1981 and the failure of state-determined needs standards to keep up with rising prices. Between 1976 and 1986 the proportion of poor persons receiving AFDC benefits fell from 45.4 percent to 34 percent (the decrease among female-headed households was even larger, from 90.1 percent to 65 percent). Non-Medicaid welfare spending fell from $0.67 to $0.37 per $100 of personal income between 1976 and 1987. AFDC accounts for about half of this decrease, but decreases in Supplemental Security Income (SSI), general assistance, and other programs targeted to the poor also occurred[33] (see Table 5.9).

The relatively small increase in health and hospital spending shown in Table 5.8 results from two offsetting trends, as Table 5.10 reveals. There was a decrease in spending for hospitals between 1976 and 1987, as it fell from $0.60 to $0.51 per $100 of personal income (15 percent), primarily as a result of the trends toward deinstitutionalization and privatization. On the other hand, health spending rose even more rapidly than hospital spending fell, increasing from $0.25 to $0.40 per $100 of personal income (60 percent), no doubt to some extent to take care of people who formerly were hospitalized. The high rate of inflation in medical costs also contributed to the growth of health spending.

Highway spending followed the same path as total spending, falling until 1983 and then rising. It was, however, more volatile than other spending, falling 28 percent and then rebounding 9 percent. The upturn after 1983 reflects growing recognition of the need to rebuild infrastructure that had been neglected during the previous fifteen years.

State aid to local governments has grown somewhat more slowly than total state spending in the 1980s, rising 67.8 percent compared to a 77 percent increase in all general state spending. Consequently, it slipped to 34.4 percent of total state spending in 1987 from 36.3 percent in 1980, its lowest level in many years. Real local aid per capita decreased in the early years of the 1980s as states struggled with serious fiscal problems and then rebounded to higher levels than prior to 1980. To some extent, the decrease in local aid has been caused by a statistical irony: when a state assumes full responsibility for a program, the aid reported by the census bureau decreases, even though the state has really relieved local governments entirely of a cost they formerly had to partially bear.[34]

The extent to which federal aid reductions have influenced state spending is not fully understood and can certainly not be interpreted well with aggregate national statistics such as those presented in this article. The most informative research on how states have responded to the reductions of federal aid has been done by two teams—one led by Richard Nathan of Princeton University and the other led by George Peterson of the Urban Institute. Nathan's research found that state responses varied considerably in the fourteen states studied. Some states replaced little if any of the federal aid with their own revenue, but others made a greater effort to restore federal aid reductions. Even the states with the largest replacement of federal funds apparently offset no more than a quarter of the federal cuts.[35]

The Urban Institute's research in eighteen states supports the findings of Nathan and his associates and uncovered many cases in which federal aid losses for particular programs were fully offset by infusions of state dollars. According to the Urban Institute's report, "the block grants can be interpreted in part as a test of states' political commitment in deciding whether or not to sustain human service programs, even when not obligated to do so by the federal government and when no longer subsidized to do so by categorical matching programs. The states passed this test of commitment to a greater degree than most observers anticipated."[36]

Richard Nathan made an additional observation along the same lines, arguing that during periods when the national government is pursuing

Table 5.11

Revenue per Pupil in 1983 and 1987 and Percentage Change Between Those Years

Revenue per pupil

State	1983		1987		Percentage change	
	Level	Rank	Level	Rank	Change	Rank
New England						
Connecticut	$3,637	6	$5,609	5	54.2%	1
Maine	2,591	37	3,586	31	38.4	10
Massachusetts	3,478	10	4,565	9	31.2	27
New Hampshire	2,781	32	3,669	29	31.9	24
Rhode Island	3,212	18	4,291	17	33.6	20
Vermont	3,088	23	4,202	18	36.1	17
Middle Atlantic						
Delaware	3,677	5	4,774	7	29.8	31
Maryland	3,405	11	4,682	8	37.5	15
New Jersey	4,303	3	6,128	3	42.4	9
New York	4,284	4	5,924	4	38.3	12
Pennsylvania	3,496	9	4,994	6	42.8	8
Great Lakes						
Illinois	3,085	24	4,119	20	33.5	21
Indiana	2,528	40	3,496	32	38.3	11
Michigan	3,145	20	3,917	24	24.6	38
Ohio	2,853	29	3,718	27	30.3	29
Wisconsin	3,325	15	4,434	10	33.3	22
Plains						
Iowa	3,092	22	3,672	28	18.7	44
Kansas	3,308	16	4,054	22	22.6	40
Minnesota	3,347	14	4,355	13	30.1	30
Missouri	2,623	36	3,454	33	31.7	26
Nebraska	2,708	35	3,413	35	26.0	36
North Dakota	3,266	17	3,366	36	3.1	48
South Dakota	2,765	33	3,346	37	21.0	43

Southeast						
Alabama	2,049	48	2,484	49	21.2	42
Arkansas	2,068	47	2,792	46	35.0	18
Florida	3,026	26	4,163	19	37.6	14
Georgia	2,292	43	3,144	40	37.1	16
Kentucky	2,297	42	3,028	41	31.8	25
Louisiana	2,723	34	3,009	42	10.5	47
Mississippi	1,922	50	2,557	48	33.0	23
North Carolina	2,260	45	3,259	39	44.2	6
South Carolina	2,267	44	3,316	38	46.3	5
Tennessee	2,041	49	2,818	44	38.0	13
Virginia	2,793	31	3,990	23	42.8	7
West Virginia	2,531	39	3,877	25	53.2	2
Southwest						
Arizona	N/A	N/A	N/A	N/A	N/A	N/A
New Mexico	3,114	21	3,661	30	17.5	45
Oklahoma	3,206	19	2,840	43	-11.4	50
Texas	2,952	27	3,855	26	30.5	28
Rocky Mountain						
Colorado	3,370	13	4,309	15	27.9	33
Idaho	2,082	46	2,661	47	27.8	34
Montana	3,521	8	4,433	11	25.9	37
Utah	2,399	41	2,804	45	16.9	46
Wyoming	5,577	1	7,159	2	28.4	32
Far West						
Alaska	5,403	2	8,214	1	32.0	3
California	2,949	28	4,383	12	48.6	4
Hawaii	3,389	12	4,300	16	46.9	35
Nevada	2,793	30	3,453	34	23.6	39
Oregon	3,560	7	4,349	14	22.2	41
Washington	3,042	25	4,106	21	35.0	19
U.S. Total	3,042		4,068		33.7	

Source: National Education Association, revision of data originally published in *Estimates of School Statistics.*

relatively conservative policies, states tend to be more liberal and activist than the national government. He notes that some conservatives were disappointed while prospending forces were heartened by the positive policies adopted by states in the 1980s.[37]

Education Spending

As noted in the previous section, education is the biggest component of state budgets. It received even more attention than usual in the 1980s because of a national wave of reform that followed publication of *A Nation at Risk*, a 1983 report by a presidential commission that viewed the state of our schools with alarm and called for a new national commitment to improving them. While *A Nation at Risk* emphasized the problems in elementary and secondary schools, higher education was receiving considerable attention because of the preoccupation with economic development and the role that universities could play in promoting the growth of jobs.

As Table 5.8 shows, education did not fare particularly well after 1983 in the competition for state budget allocations. To some extent, this is because enrollment was relatively flat. Elementary-secondary enrollment finally bottomed out in 1984–85 following a 14.4 percent decrease from 1973, but it rose a mere 2.0 percent over the next three years. Enrollment is still falling at the secondary level although in most states it is rising at the elementary level. Higher education enrollment also was relatively stagnant, trending moderately higher from 1976 to 1983, then decreasing slightly for two years, and rebounding slightly in 1986 and 1987. The total increase between 1976 and 1987 was less than 5 percent.[38]

States have gradually been assuming a larger share of the cost of elementary-secondary schools. By the 1987–88 school year states were providing 49.8 percent of total school revenue (53.1 percent of non-federal school revenue). This is the highest proportion ever and compares to 44.3 percent ten years earlier. Despite the increase in the state share, local revenue is still important. Nationally, it accounted for close to 40 percent of the new money flowing to schools in 1986, 1987, and 1988. States that gave local governments a significant role in increasing school funding were generally among the leaders in increasing total school revenue.[39]

As Table 5.11 demonstrates, the experiences of different states vary tremendously, with Connecticut boosting revenue per pupil 76 percent between 1983 and 1988 while six states had increases of 20 percent or less in that period. Several factors help to account for these differences:

- *State fiscal condition.* States with strong finances tended to have bigger increases.
- *Enrollment changes.* States with declining enrollments were in a better position to boost per pupil expenditures.
- *Priorities.* Some of the states with relatively low spending made special efforts to boost the resources for schools. Examples include Indiana, North Carolina, South Carolina, and Virginia.

Only a small number of states raised their taxes significantly to improve their educational systems. All of these states previously had relatively low levels of support for the schools, including Arkansas, Indiana, Kentucky, Maine, South Carolina, Tennessee, and Texas.

Florida, North Carolina, and Virginia boosted school resources substantially without increasing state taxes for that purpose by squeezing the share of the budget going for other programs or by mandating large increases in local school taxes. In general, however, the unwillingness to raise state taxes seriously limited the additional resources that could be devoted to schools.

The revenue increases were substantial in absolute terms: revenue per pupil rose 41 percent between 1982–83 and 1987–88 while inflation was 25 percent. But such increases were nowhere near large enough to fund the great improvement in quality envisioned by many of the school reformers.[40]

To a substantial extent, much of the energy of the states went into low-cost measures to improve the schools—raising standards for teacher education, requiring that pupils achieve higher norms in order to graduate, increasing the use of testing, enhancing accountability, and so forth. A large proportion of the additional funds went for higher teacher salaries, but much of the salary gain in the 1983–88 period merely offset the erosion of salaries in the previous five years.[41]

At the higher education level one of the most important trends was a shift to increased reliance on tuition as a means of financing state universities and colleges. Between 1981 and 1988, the average tuitions at state universities and state colleges rose 93.3 percent and 91.7 percent, respectively. By contrast, state appropriations increased only 62.6 percent. In other words, students are now shouldering a considerably larger share of the cost of their education. This contrasts with the trend in the 1970s, when appropriations increases significantly outpaced tuition growth.[42] The major reasons for this shift are the weakened fiscal condition of the states and the stronger competition for state appropriations from other parts of the state budget.

Outlook for the Next Decade

The course of state fiscal policy in the 1990s depends on developments in four areas—the health of the economy, federal budget and tax policy, taxpayer willingness to pay higher taxes, and service demands. While the surprising developments of the period since 1978 instill a high level of caution in anyone trying to predict the future, probabilities favor the next decade being no better than the past five years, and the odds are that it will be a period of considerable fiscal stress.

Although this discussion generalizes about trends for all states, there are certain to be wide differences among the states. No matter what happens to the national economy, some regions invariably experience stronger growth than others. The fortunes of the states will also vary for reasons such as demographics and the soundness of their tax systems.

The Economy

After getting off to a poor start in the first years of the decade, the economy performed extremely well after 1983. We are in the midst of the longest peacetime recovery in our history and have far surpassed the previous record for an economic expansion. It is not likely that the next five years will be as prosperous as the past five years for most states. With the economy already at virtually full employment, economic growth is constrained by the growth of capacity. Since capacity will expand with productivity growth and the labor force, neither of which is increasing rapidly, relatively slow growth is the best that can occur.

Several economic dangers lie in wait. To reduce the trade deficit, policy makers may attempt to depress domestic demand to reduce imports and provide room for increasing exports. To reduce the budget deficit, federal spending may be cut and taxes increased. Unless deficit reduction is accompanied by easier monetary policy, it could cause a recession. But can the U.S. relax its monetary policy without a coordinated easing worldwide? If there is a recession, it could be a severe one because the high level of private indebtedness tends to increase instability.

The United States no longer is the master of its own economic fate to the extent that it used to be. With the increased level of economic interdependence among the major economic powers, monetary and fiscal policy are not as effective as they once were. The level of long-term interest rates, for example, may depend more on decisions in Tokyo, London, and Zurich than at the Federal Reserve Board. This implies that it will be more difficult to extricate ourselves from a difficult economic position when we encounter one.

Federal Budget and Tax Policy

The most likely initiatives from Washington would harm the states fiscally. The question is: to what extent?

Aid to state and local governments has borne the brunt of much of the federal budget tightening during the 1980s. As the budget submitted by President Reagan in January 1989 reported, aid to states and localities (excluding payments for individuals, such as Medicaid and AFDC) was reduced 37 percent in real terms between 1980 and 1988.[43] But, as was discussed above, the greatest losses were suffered by localities rather than states, and the worst damage was done in 1981, with later Reagan proposals to cut aid having considerably less success than those in his first year in office.

It is conceivable that the federal government could get tougher on the states in the 1990s. The most damaging policy would be to force states to pay a greater proportion of Medicaid. There are signs that forces are developing in Washington to adopt more activist domestic policies. One way to do that without enlarging the federal deficit would be to enact or enlarge unfunded mandates on states and localities. A harbinger of what may occur is the catastrophic health, welfare reform, and nursing home legislation enacted in recent years, which collectively add significantly to state health costs through new mandates.

The irony of such policies is that they would lead to state and local tax increases even as they avoided federal increases. The federal government also could add to state revenue problems by increasing excise taxes, particularly on motor fuels and tobacco products, which would reduce state revenue from those sources and inhibit future increases. An even worse policy from the states' viewpoint would be a federal value added tax, since it would be an incursion into the consumption tax field that the states have had to themselves, making it more difficult for states to boost sales tax rates. As noted above, the sales tax is still the largest state revenue source.

Taxpayer Willingness to Pay Higher Taxes

If recent patterns continue, states will generally avoid major tax increases until they have endured a period of fiscal stress during which they have tightened spending and perhaps enacted some minor tax increases and accounting devices to postpone the need for raising taxes. Inhibitions about raising taxes are in part a legacy of the tax revolt of the late 1970s and in part a result of the high level of intergovernmental competition in the 1980s.

A major unanswered question is whether significant tax increases can be sold in the absence of such a fiscal crisis. It is conceivable that strong political leadership will convince the public that taxes need to be raised to improve the level of services, particularly for education and transportation. That is, however, unlikely, expect in states where the quality of public services clearly lags behind the national average. Unless it does occur, the recent pattern of taxes remaining relatively steady as a proportion of personal income will probably continue. In view of the prevailing budgetary pressures and the low probability of significantly cutting back existing programs, this would preclude states undertaking costly new initiatives.

Service Demands

The large recent increases in Medicaid and corrections costs show no sign of abating. States are also moving in the direction of assuming court costs from localities, and momentum is building for improved services for children, especially in their preschool years (both day care and early childhood education).

A major issue in the future is the extent to which states will provide services for senior citizens who will be increasing in number rapidly. Aside from long-term care, state and local governments do not devote much of their budgets to the elderly at the present time. This will be a growing issue in the future, but the major impact will not be felt until the twenty-first century, when the baby boomers reach retirement age.

Summary and Conclusions

The most probable outlook for the states is for increasing fiscal stress. The economy is likely to perform worse than it has in the past five years, federal policy will probably impose additional burdens, the existing demands will not slacken, and some new demands may intensify.

The decade ahead will probably provide new challenges. As the federal government continues to retrench, states will need to find better ways to economize and make the system more efficient. This ought to include not only streamlining state programs but also reassessing policies toward local governments and reshaping them to improve the operation of a federal system with a diminished role for the federal government.[44]

The record since 1975 also offers a basis for optimism in that state and local governments successfully surmounted a long list of problems—the New York City fiscal crisis, the tax revolt, the most severe recessions since the 1930s, and sharp federal aid cutbacks. The system proved itself very resilient, and states were widely applauded for the manner in which they shouldered their enhanced responsibilities.[45]

Appendix
Methodology and Sources for Estimates of Spending and Federal Aid

The starting point for measuring state government spending and federal aid is the series of reports published annually by the U.S. Census Bureau, *State Government Finances in (year)*. This information was augmented by data from several additional sources to compensate for limitations of the Census data.

Total spending in Table 5.8 is general state spending as reported by the census bureau, with federal aid subtracted.

Higher education spending is state appropriations for higher education as reported by Illinois State University in its monthly publication, *The Grapevine*, as reproduced in John R. Wittstruck and Stephen M. Bragg, *Focus on Price* (Denver: State Higher Education Executive Officers, 1988), p. 49. This measure abstracts from revenue from tuition and other charges as well as all activities of auxiliary enterprises.

Spending for elementary-secondary education is from National Education Association, *Estimates of School Statistics: 1987–88* and previous issues. It includes not only aid to school districts but also state contributions to teacher retirement systems.

Medicaid spending is from Congressional Research Service, *Medicaid Sourcebook: Background Data and Analysis* (November 1988), pp. 29–30. Since that data is for calendar years, fiscal year figures were estimated by averaging calendar years. The CRS data does not distinguish between state and local Medicaid spending, so information from the census bureau's annual reports on city and county finances were used to eliminate nonstate Medicaid spending. Only partial information was available from that source for years prior to 1978. Spending in 1987 was estimated from information provided by the U.S. Health Care Financing Administration.

Other welfare spending was estimated by subtracting Medicaid spending from the total spending on welfare reported by the U.S. Census Bureau.

Spending for health, hospitals, highways, and corrections was taken directly from the Census Bureau's reports. Note that it includes spending from charges, which was excluded for other kinds of spending, so Table 5.7 exaggerates its relative size in comparison with other parts of state budgets.

Other spending is (a) expenditures reported by the census bureau other than for the spending categories itemized in the table and (b) the difference between Census education spending and spending included in the table.

Federal aid was taken from census bureau reports except for Medicaid, which is from U.S. Office of Management and Budget, *Budget of the United States: Historical Tables: Fiscal Year 1989*.

Personal income is from U.S. Commerce Department, *Survey of Current Business* (August 1987).

Notes

1. Two econometric analyses have found a statistically significant difference in state fiscal behavior before and after 1978 or 1980. Peter D. Skaperdas, "Quantifying State and Local Government Discretionary Policy Changes," in "State and Local Governments: An Assessment of Their Financial Position and Fiscal Policies," Federal Reserve Bank of New York, *Quarterly Review* (Winter 1983/84), and Roy Bahl and William Duncombe, "State and Local Government Finances: Was There a Structural Break in the Reagan Years?" unpublished ms. The latter article was unable to differentiate between 1978 and 1980 as the turning point.

2. State tax revenue in the year ending June 1988 was $262 billion, according

to the U.S. Census Bureau's quarterly *Summary of Federal, State, and Local Tax Revenue* (April-June 1988). Since it has surely risen more than 3 percent since then, it is currently above $270 billion.

3. The only states with other fiscal years are Alabama and Michigan (ending September 30), Texas (August 31), and New York (March 31).

4. Steven D. Gold, "Recent Developments in State Finances," *National Tax Journal* (March 1983), 1–29; idem. "Tax Increases of 1983: Prelude to Another Tax Revolt?" *National Tax Journal* (March 1984), 9–22.

5. Twelve out of seventeen personal income tax increases enacted in 1982 or 1983 were rolled back, repealed, or allowed to expire. In contrast, most of the sales tax increases enacted in those years remained in effect. Steven D. Gold, "Developments in State Finances, 1983 to 1986," *Public Budgeting and Finance* (Spring 1987), 20–21. That article omitted an income tax increase in Colorado that did remain in effect.

6. Even though the period from 1983 to 1988 was the longest peacetime economic expansion in history, the growth of real incomes was not particularly impressive by historical standards. Many households had to rely on two earners to maintain their desired standard of living. Real earnings rose relatively slowly because of the sluggish growth rate of productivity.

7. Steven D. Gold, *Property Tax Relief* (Lexington, MA: D.C. Heath, 1979).

8. These figures are from the U.S. Census Bureau's annual publication, *Government Finances in* (year). If contributions to Social Security and other social insurance programs are included, the relative increase in state taxes appears less significant.

9. John Mikesell, "Reforming and Restructuring State General Sales Taxes: What Now?" paper presented at the conference of the Association for Public Policy Analysis and Management, Seattle, WA (October 1988).

10. For a contrast of trends in state and federal corporation income taxes, see Robert McIntyre, "Are States Overtaxing Or Undertaxing Corporations," in *The Unfinished Agenda for State Tax Reform*, Steven D. Gold, ed., 197–217 (Denver: National Conference of State Legislatures, 1988).

11. For a review of trends in state corporate tax revenue, see Robert Aten and Steven Gold, "Where's the Corporate Windfall?" *Tax Notes* (October 2, 1989), 107–114.

12. The eight states where severance taxes account for the highest proportion of tax revenue are Alaska, Louisiana, Montana, New Mexico, North Dakota, Oklahoma, Texas, and Wyoming.

13. For additional analysis of how state tax trends differed among the states between 1970 and 1987, see Steven Gold and Judy Zelio, "Interstate Tax Comparisons and How They Have Changed Over Time," *Tax Notes* (March 20, 1989), 1501–1512.

14. In November 1978, Idaho voters approved a Proposition 13 clone, which was statutory rather than constitutional. It was amended by law before it took effect.

15. In the three cases in which voters approved radical tax-cutting measures the situation was perceived as "out of control." In all cases, there were sharp increases (California and Idaho) or else the level of taxes was particularly high (Massachusetts). Gold, "Tax Increases of 1983."

16. In 1987, miscellaneous revenue consisted of interest (49.2 percent), rents and royalties (18.6 percent), donations (6.3 percent), fines and forfeits (2.7 percent),

sales of property (0.6 percent), and other types of revenue (22.6 percent).

17. Steven D. Gold, "The Blizzard of 1987: A Year of Tax Reform Activity in the States," *Publius* 18 (Summer 1988), 17–35.

18. In terms of federal fiscal years, there was also a decrease in aid in 1987, primarily because of the termination of General Revenue Sharing. That decrease does not occur in U.S. Census Bureau statistics, which use state and local fiscal years; census statistics indicate a small increase in 1987.

19. Richard P. Nathan and John R. Lago, "Intergovernmental Relations in the Reagan Era," *Public Budgeting and Finance* 8 (Autumn 1988), 15–29.

20. Ibid.

21. For a review of estimates of the fungibility of federal aid to state and local governments, see U.S. Treasury Department, *Federal-State-Local Fiscal Relations* (Washington, DC: USGPO, 1985), pp. 161–67. Unfortunately, the econometric research reviewed deals with the period of rising federal aid rather than the 1980s, when the real value of federal aid was decreasing.

22. Revenue sharing represented 1.0 percent of state general revenue in 1980 and 1.2 percent of local general revenue in 1986; as a proportion of tax revenue, it was 1.7 percent and 3.1 percent, respectively.

23. Edward M. Gramlich made such an inference in a review of state and local revenue changes between 1980 and 1986. See his "Federalism and Federal Deficit Reduction," *National Tax Journal* xi (September 1987), 303.

24. Some of the interest revenue reflected arbitrage activity and was balanced by higher interest expenditures; other interest revenue was related to expanded activities in mortgage subsidies and other programs involving sinking funds. Most of the revenue from oil royalties flowed to a small number of states, and much of it was dedicated to permanent funds.

25. William F. Fox and Charles Campbell, "Stability of the State Sales Tax Elasticity," *National Tax Journal* xxxvii (June 1984), 201–212.

26. Steven D. Gold, "Intergovernmental Competition and State Income Taxes," in a forthcoming book on intergovernmental competition edited by Daphne Kenyon to be published by the Urban Institute; Harvey Galper and Stephen Pollack, "Models of State Income Tax Reform," in *The Unfinished Agenda for State Tax Reform*, Steven D. Gold, ed., 107–128 (Denver: National Conference of State Legislatures, 1988), demonstrates that 1987 tax reforms tended to reduce elasticity.

27. Because states have improved their cash management practices, they do not need to hold as high balances for transactions purposes as in the past. Consequently, a larger proportion of balances now are for precautionary purposes.

Another indicator of fiscal stress, aside from the balances held, is the number of states reducing their budgets after the fiscal year has started. Such reductions are common when states experience revenue shortfalls. The number of reductions was 21 in 1982, 39 in 1983, 3 in 1985, 18 in 1986, and 24 in 1987. The number in 1984 is not available. Corina L. Eckl, *State Deficit Management Strategies* (Denver: National Conference of State Legislatures, 1987).

28. Steven D. Gold, Corina L. Eckl, and Martha Fabricius, *State Budget Actions in 1988* (Denver: National Conference of State Legislatures, 1988).

Table 5.7 is based upon reports published by the National Association of State Budget Officers (NASBO) rather than National Conference of State Legislatures (NCSL), even though there are some differences in the way the two groups classify Rainy Day Funds (RDFs). NCSL reports higher national RDF balances because

NASBO does not include balances in certain states, such as California, where most of the year-end General Fund balance automatically goes into its budget stabilization fund. The reason why NASBO figures are used in this chapter is that NASBO reports revised estimates approximately nine months after the end of the fiscal year, which are more accurate than NCSL's estimates, which are reported at the end of the fiscal year.

29. A small amount of federal aid is included for corrections spending. Higher education includes only state appropriations, not the spending paid for from tuitions. Spending financed by charges is, however, included in other spending categories. See the Appendix for a description of the methodology and sources used to derive these estimates.

30. At least thirty-six states are under court order to improve conditions in their correctional facilities.

31. For a good description of factors driving up Medicaid costs and how state programs differ, see Congressional Research Service, *Medicaid SourceBook: Background Data and Analysis* (November 1988).

32. U.S. Committee on Ways and Means, House of Representatives, *Background Material and Data on Programs Within the Jurisdiction of the Committee on Ways and Means: 1988 Edition* (March 24, 1988), p. 417. Between 1972 and 1986, Maine was the only state where AFDC and food stamp benefits kept up with inflation. Since food stamps are indexed to inflation, it was the real decrease in AFDC benefits that caused the reduction. There were only five states where the decrease during that period was less than 10 percent. U.S. ACIR, *Significant Features of Fiscal Federalism, 1987 Edition* (Washington, DC: USGPO), p. 126.

33. The census bureau does not provide sufficient detail to determine specifically all of the factors that contributed to the decrease in welfare spending. It defines public welfare spending as "support of and assistance to needy persons contingent upon their need." The portion of welfare spending that is not for cash assistance to persons or vendor payments for medical care has decreased substantially since 1976. In that year, state welfare spending of $29.6 billion included $5.6 billion for cash assistance, $11 billion for medical vendor payments, and $13 billion for other programs. In 1987, total welfare spending of $78.4 billion included $22.1 billion for cash assistance, $38.5 billion for medical vendor payments, and only $17.9 billion for other programs. Unless there was some change in Census Bureau procedures, this is a highly significant development. U.S. Census Bureau, *State Government Finances in 1976*, p. 8; U.S. Census Bureau, *State Government Finances in 1987* (Washington, DC: USGPO), pp. 4, 64.

34. For a detailed analysis of changes in state aid between 1980 and 1986, see Steven D. Gold and Brenda M. Erickson, "State Aid to Local Governments in the 1980s," *State and Local Government Review* (Winter 1989), 11–32.

35. Richard P. Nathan, Fred C. Doolittle, and Associates, *Reagan and the States* (Princeton: Princeton University Press, 1987).

36. George E. Peterson et. al., *The Reagan Block Grants* (Washington DC: The Urban Institute, 1986), p. 15.

37. Richard P. Nathan, "The Role of the States in American Federalism," in *State of the States* (Washington, DC: Congressional Quarterly, 1988).

38. The change in elementary-secondary enrollment is for the Fall semester as reported by National Education Association (NEA), *Estimates of School Statistics* (Washington, DC: various years). Higher education enrollment was provided by

Jacqueline Johnson of the State of Washington, Higher Education Coordinating Board. These statistics estimate full-time equivalent enrollment by treating each three part-time students as the equivalent of one full-time student.

39. Steven D. Gold, *Recent Trends in Financing Elementary and Secondary Schools* (Denver: NCSL, 1989).

40. Ibid.

41. According to NEA, the average classroom teacher had a salary increase of only 7.3 percent in the decade ending in 1987–88, after eliminating the effects of inflation. There was a sharp decrease in the inflation-adjusted salary from 1977–78 to 1979–80 and little change the following two years. From 1981–82 to 1987–88, the real increase was 18.5 percent. NEA, *Estimates, 1987–88*, pp. 16–17.

42. John R. Wittstruck and Stephen M. Bragg, *Focus on Price* (Denver: State Higher Education Executive Officers, 1988).

43. U.S. Office of Management and Budget, *Budget of the United States Government: Fiscal Year 1990* (Washington, DC: USGPO, 1989), pp. 2a–12.

44. National Conference of State Legislatures's Task Force on State-Local Relations has laid out a blueprint for how such a reform of state-local relations might evolve. See its *Recommendations* (Denver: National Conference of State Legislatures, 1986).

45. This point has been emphasized by John Shannon, former executive director of the U.S. ACIR.

—————— 6 ——————

Big City Finances in the New Era of Fiscal Federalism

HELEN F. LADD

New York City's financial crisis in 1975 focused national and worldwide attention on the fiscal problems of U.S. cities. Like many other older cities, New York suffered from the failure of its tax base to grow in line with the revenue needs of an increasingly dependent population and from the adverse effects on its budget of inflation and recession. Also like many other older cities, its heavy reliance on intergovernmental assistance made it vulnerable to reductions in external aid. Poor fiscal health turned to financial crisis, and ultimately to the need for an emergency federal loan, when city officials responded to the 1974–75 recession and a slowdown in intergovernmental assistance largely by borrowing rather than by raising taxes or decreasing spending. With much of this additional borrowing in the form of short-term debt, the crisis was triggered when investors lost confidence in the city's ability to repay its loans.

For the first few years after New York's financial crisis, big cities throughout the country benefited from the expansion of the national economy and the injection of new countercyclical aid. However, federal aid to state and local governments peaked in 1978 and two years later the economy slid into recession. After a brief recovery, the economy deteriorated again and the country entered its worst recession since the Depression. Simultaneously, cities experienced significant new cutbacks in federal aid at the hands of the Reagan administration and faced local

This paper was completed while the author was a Visiting Scholar at the Federal Reserve Bank of Boston. It draws heavily on the material in Helen F. Ladd, "Big City Finances" to be published under the auspices of the Taubman Center for State and Local Governments, Kennedy School of Government, Harvard University. The author thanks the Ford Foundation for financial assistance for the larger project. This paper also draws on Helen F. Ladd and John Yinger, *America's Ailing Cities* (Baltimore: Johns Hopkins University Press, 1989).

voters who were reluctant to pay higher taxes. By the end of 1982, the economy began to recover, but federal assistance to cities continued to fall. The recession, high interest rates, a nationwide tax revolt, and loss of federal aid presented major new challenges for city governments in the early 1980s and raised the specter of financial crises in other big cities. But, in fact, America's big cities muddled through the fiscal challenges of the early 1980s with no serious financial crises.

However, the absence of financial crises does not mean that big cities are in strong fiscal health. Indeed, a main theme of this paper is that the capacity of cities to provide adequate public services to their residents at reasonable tax rates has been declining over time. After a brief summary of the recent changes in cities' fiscal environment, the paper first examines changes in the financial or budgetary condition of big cities, then turns to changes in city tax burdens and service levels, and, finally, analyzes changes in their underlying fiscal health. The paper shows that the fiscal health of many big cities has been deteriorating over time and concludes that many cities will need additional state or federal assistance to provide adequate public services at reasonable tax rates.

Impediments to Raising Revenue

In his excellent 1976 comprehensive study of big city finances, George Peterson of the Urban Institute asserted that 1975 would be remembered "for its rediscovery of the budget constraint."[1] During the 1960s and early 1970s, cities had behaved as if they were not constrained. Spending by big city governments had grown dramatically, fueled largely by the growth of federal assistance. Between 1962 and 1972, spending by the twenty-eight largest cities (including that of their overlying school districts) nearly tripled and grew about 20 percent faster than the state and local public sector at the time when that sector was increasing its share of Gross National Product by 40 percent.[2]

During the following decade, spending by big cities slowed down both absolutely and relative to that of all state and local governments as cities faced new impediments to financing public services. These impediments took the form of cutbacks in federal aid and the demise of the federal-local partnership, the vigorous opposition of taxpayers throughout the country to increased state and local taxes, and the increased difficulty of raising funds through the municipal bond market. In 1986, cities were faced with another change in federal policy that is likely to exacerbate their future fiscal problems, namely, the Tax Reform Act of that year.

The End of the Federal-Local Partnership

During the 1960s and early 1970s, two different philosophies had motivated the growth of direct federal assistance to cities. First, federal policy
makers believed that cities needed narrowly defined categorical aid to
meet the needs of their impoverished residents.

Recognizing a collection of unmet needs in urban areas, such as
inadequate housing and transportation, deteriorating neighborhoods,
high crime, failing schools, and limited job opportunities, especially for
minorities, and believing that cities had neither the financial nor the
political capacity to deal with these needs, federal policy makers provided categorical aid for an assortment of new programs, such as neighborhood health care, legal aid, and manpower training. In contrast, the
1972 introduction of general revenue sharing was motivated by the view
that the superior revenue-raising capacity of the federal government
should be harnessed to provide no-strings-attached aid to state and local
governments to use as they pleased. The categorical programs together
with revenue sharing resulted in a dramatic upsurge in direct federal
assistance to cities.

Neither philosophy survived into the 1980s. During the Reagan years,
cities were no longer viewed as the deserving level of government, and
huge federal deficits left no surplus revenues for state and local governments.[3] As early as 1974, federal assistance to cities had begun to level
off. But the underlying trend in federal assistance was not fully perceived
because of a temporary surge in the late 1970s in federal jobs programs
and countercyclical assistance provided through the Comprehensive
Employment and Training Act (CETA), Anti-Recession Fiscal Assistance (ARFA), and Emergency Local Public Works. Federal aid to cities,
and also to all state and local governments, peaked in 1978. The elimination of the countercyclical programs and the leveling of other programs
halted the twelve-year growth in federal aid to cities even before the 1980
election of President Reagan. President Reagan's budget cutting agenda
greatly accelerated the decline as various categorical programs for cities
were consolidated into block grants to states, programs of special importance to urban governments were slashed, and revenue sharing was
eliminated in 1986. The fall from grace of the cities during the Reagan
years is demonstrated by the fact that aid programs for urban areas

declined by 47 percent between 1980 and 1987 at the same time that all other federal grant programs (including Aid For Dependent Children—AFDC—and Medicaid) experienced a 47 percent increase.[4]

By 1982, federal aid to all cities had declined to 18.4 percent of own-source revenue, its level in the early 1970s, and by 1986 it had declined further to under 12 percent. Moreover huge federal budget deficits, combined with the 1985 Gramm-Rudman mechanism to reduce them, portend no turnaround in the downward trend. Thus, the 1977–86 decade witnessed a major change in federal-city relations. During this period, the federal government made it clear that it would no longer serve as the funding source for increased city spending and that it would no longer provide aid to alleviate the fiscal stress of cities during recessions. Instead the cities were left to fend for themselves or to rely on assistance from their states.

The Tax Revolt

But the late 1970s and early 1980s was not a good time for cities to rely more heavily on their own revenue or that of their states. Spurred on by the success at the polls of California's Proposition 13, taxpayer voters across the country joined the tax revolt bandwagon and passed referenda to limit state or local taxes or both in many states and made elected public officials more reluctant to vote for tax increases. This national tax revolt lowered total state and local taxes from 11.5 percent of personal income in 1977 to 10.3 percent in 1982.

Cutbacks in federal aid and the tax revolt also affected state governments and thereby diminished their ability to assist big cities. Consequently, the average big city adjusted to the decline in federal aid on the revenue side almost entirely by increasing the share of revenues from its own sources (see Table 6.1). The percentage of general city revenues from the federal government in the average big city declined from 20 percent in 1977 to 10 percent in 1986 while the share from own sources increased from 61 to 71 percent. During this same time period, the share of city revenue from state governments decreased from 16.6 to 16.1 percent. Only in thirteen big cities did the share of revenue from the state government increase during this period and in most of them the increase was not sufficient to offset the decline in federal aid. One exception was Boston where additional state aid partially compensated the city for its loss of property tax revenues under Massachusetts's stringent tax limitation measure.

Table 6.1

Mix of Revenues—1977, 1982, 1986
(thirty-three big cities)

	1977	1982	1986
Percentage of general revenues from			
Federal govern-			
ment	20.2	16.4	10.1
State government	16.6	16.6	16.1
Other local			
governments	2.3	2.2	3.3
Own sources	60.8	64.8	70.5
Percentage of own-source revenues from			
Taxes	68.4	61.2	59.4
Charges	20.2	20.9	20.7
Miscellaneous			
(not interest)	5.5	6.5	9.4
Interest	5.4	11.4	10.5
Percentage of taxes from			
Property	55.2	48.0	47.5
General sales	11.8	13.7	13.0
Selected sales	11.5	14.4	14.5
Income	13.8	15.6	16.2
Other	7.7	8.4	8.7

Source: U.S. Department of Commerce, Bureau of the Census, City Government Finances, 1977, 1982, and 1986 (Washington, DC: U.S. Government Printing Office).

Note: Simple unweighted averages for thirty-three big cities. For list of cities, see note 8.

Turbulence in the Municipal Bond Market

Historically, cities raised about 50 percent of their funds for capital projects by issuing bonds in the municipal—or tax-exempt—bond market. During the 1970s, this proportion declined with the increased availability of intergovernmental aid, primarily from the federal government, for capital projects. With the fall in federal aid, cities were expected to increase their reliance on the municipal bond market.

However, the early 1980s witnessed turbulence in the municipal bond market as interest rates on tax-exempt bonds escalated, both absolutely and relative to comparable taxable bonds. In 1982, for example, interest rates on high grade municipal bonds rose to 11.57 percent, only 11 percent below the rate of return on taxable U.S. Treasury securities. The combined effects of record interest rates on long term bonds and the tax revolt made it increasingly difficult for city officials to garner support for general obligation bonds to finance capital projects. Instead they turned increasingly to various forms of creative financing, including sale leasebacks, to revenue bonds which do not require a public vote, and to special authorities that could issue revenue bonds financed by user charges. Between 1977 and 1986, the typical big city decreased the share of its general purpose debt backed by the full faith and credit of the city from 69 percent of all new general purpose debt to 44 percent. Only by shifting to nonguaranteed bonds were cities able to raise much money through the municipal bond market.

Federal Tax Reform

In 1986, big cities were faced with another major change in federal policy, in the form of the Tax Reform Act, that could adversely affect their future ability to raise revenue. This landmark legislation reduced individual tax rates, eliminated the deductibility of state and local sales taxes, and placed new restrictions on borrowing through the tax-exempt bond market. The fact that sales taxes alone are no longer deductible may encourage cities that use sales taxes to alter the mix of their taxes somewhat in favor of other deductible local taxes. In addition, the restrictions on tax-exempt borrowing and the fall in the value of tax exemption because of the lower federal tax rates are likely to encourage some cities to reduce their debt issues, to increase the use of current revenues to finance capital projects, to require developers to underwrite more of the costs of infrastructure, and to make more use of (the more expensive) taxable bond market.[5]

Two indirect effects are likely to be important for those cities, such as many in the Northeast and Midwest, that are located in jurisdictionally fragmented metropolitan areas. By returning a portion of their tax payments in the form of lower federal taxes, deductibility of state and local taxes serves as a bribe to keep high-income households in high tax rate, low-income jurisdictions. The tax reform act reduces the value of this bribe and may reduce city tax bases by encouraging middle and high income households to move out of central cities. In addition, cities will be hurt if state governments respond to federal tax reform either by curtailing the total amount of aid to local governments or by redirecting state aid away from central cities toward suburban areas. This latter outcome would occur if state policymakers respond to political pressures from high income suburban itemizers who face the largest increases in the net burden of state taxes as a result of federal tax reform.[6]

Cause for Concern

The combination of cutbacks in federal aid, recession, high interest rates, and the tax revolt raised serious concerns in the early 1980s about the ability of cities to cope. However, some observers have concluded that cities survived these pressures surprisingly well and were in remarkably strong fiscal condition in the early 1980s. In a recent study for the Committee on National Urban Policy of the National Research Council, Philip Dearborn concluded that

> as of 1984 [the major cities] were in perhaps the best financial condition they had been in since 1971, as judged by their success in balancing budgets and maintaining balance-sheet surpluses and liquidity. This favorable condition can be expected to continue for most major cities, as least as long as the national economy remains healthy.[7]

But this conclusion was overly sanguine and, more importantly, was based on cities' short run budgetary or financial condition, with little attention to what was happening to city service levels and tax rates. In the following sections, we look first at changes over time in cities' short run financial condition, then turn to tax rates and service levels, and finally to longer run trends in their underlying ability to provide adequate services at reasonable tax rates.

Financial Management

A city has a weak financial condition if its current expenditures continually exceed its current revenues, it relies excessively on short-term debt, or it has difficulty meeting its cash needs. This budgetary or financial perspective, which is the focus of this section, is important because it is the context within which most local government spending and financing decisions are made in the short run. However, one should be careful not to interpret an improvement in a city's budgetary condition as an improvement in the city's fiscal health, that is, in the underlying tradeoff the city faces between lower taxes and more publicly provided goods and services.

Putting aside the specific pressures associated with recession, the budgetary or financial condition of big cities has apparently strengthened over time, but only modestly and not for all cities. This conclusion is based on a comparison of various financial measures for thirty-three big cities during two comparable three-year periods.[8] The periods 1977–79 and 1984–86 are similar in terms of how they relate to the economic cycle. Both periods begin two years after a recession (the 1974–75 recession in the former case and the 1981–82 recession in the latter case) and encompass years of economic expansion. Thus the data should be free of the effects of recession, and, because they cover three years, make it possible to distinguish long-term trends from short-term aberrations.

More Conservative Financial Management

Average budgetary surpluses in the thirty-three big cities were slightly higher in the later three-year period than in the earlier period. Specifically, the average general purpose surplus for these cities rose from about 13.5 percent of expenditures in the 1977–79 period to over 14.5 percent in the 1984–86 period.[9] Although not large, the fact that this increase occurred when federal aid was falling is noteworthy. Despite such cutbacks, or perhaps because of them, cities appear to be managing their budgets more conservatively. Cities also appear to be managing their pension plans for city employees more responsibly. Historically, many city pension plans were operated on a pay-as-you-go basis, but recently cities have been putting more money aside annually in a fund to meet future liabilities. Boston changed its behavior the most during the period, increasing its contributions from 6 percent of wages and salaries in 1977 to 23 percent in 1986. Other cities such as Cincinnati, Memphis, Miami, Milwaukee, Jacksonville, and Chicago also significantly increased their contributions.

In addition, cities seem to have learned from New York City's 1975 financial crisis of the potential dangers of extensive use of short-term debt. Although the average amount of short-term debt outstanding at the end of the fiscal year has remained relatively constant as a share of general revenue over time, the number of big cities with such debt declined from 24 cities in 1977 to 17 in 1986. Several cities such as Detroit, New York, Pittsburgh, and Seattle that made significant use of

Table 6.2

Budget Balances over Time

Big cities with low budget surplus in at least two of three years

A. In both early period (1977–79) and late period (1984–86)

Boston	Minneapolis
Chicago	New York
Cleveland	Philadelphia
Detroit	Pittsburgh
Miami	San Antonio
Milwaukee	Washington, DC

B. In early period (1977–79) only

Columbus
Memphis
St. Louis

C. In late period (1984–86) only

San Francisco
Seattle
Portland

Source: U.S. Department of Commerce, Bureau of the Census, *City Government Finances*, various years (Washington, DC: U.S. Government Printing Office).

Notes: The budget surplus is calculated as total general purpose revenues minus general purpose current account expenditures divided by expenditures. Total revenue includes both own source and intergovernmental revenue. Total expenditures are general expenditures minus capital outlays plus long-term debt retired (adjusted for refunding) plus contributions to city retirement systems. A low budget surplus is less than 10 percent of expenditures.

short-term debt in 1977 apparently changed their ways and reduced their reliance on such debt to more manageable levels in many of the other five years. Although extensive use of short-term debt continues to be common practice in many big cities, cities in the aggregate appear to have become somewhat more conservative about their use of such debt.

Continuing Budgetary Pressure

However, improvement over time in the financial condition of big cities should not be overstated. Many cities that faced budgetary pressure in the earlier period also faced such pressure in the later period. Table 6.2 lists the cities that had low general purpose surpluses in each period. Based on a cutoff of 10 percent, twelve of the thirty-three cities had low or negative surpluses during at least two years in both periods. Thus, budgetary problems in many cities have persisted over time. Three cities that had low surpluses in the 1970s, Columbus, Memphis, and St. Louis, showed some improvement according to this measure over time. In contrast, three Western cities, Portland, Seattle, and San Francisco, experienced more severe budgetary pressures in the 1980s than in the 1970s. Thus, we find a stubborn persistence of budgetary pressures in more than a third of America's big cities and emerging budgetary problems in a few Western cities.

Capital Spending and Bond Ratings as Indicators of Budgetary Pressure

Changes over time in capital spending as a percent of general purpose spending also indicate a somewhat bleaker picture. Cities that are facing budgetary pressure are more likely than those without such pressure to reduce their spending on capital projects such as roads, bridges, and buildings, because the short run effects of such cuts are less visible than are cuts in services such as public safety. Between 1977 and 1986, the typical big city decreased its capital spending from 20 to 16 percent of its general purpose spending. This decline is consistent with the view that cities faced significant budgetary pressure during the period.

A final indicator of changes in the financial condition of big cities is changes in their bond ratings over time. Moody's Investors Service grounds its rating on a city's economic base, measures of indebtedness, administration factors, and financial factors. Hence, a city's rating reflects more than just current financial condition. Nonetheless, bond ratings partially reflect such conditions. Moreover, they directly affect those conditions; by raising the cost of current borrowing, a downgrading of a city's general obligation bond rating increases the pressure on a city's current budget.

Table 6.3 lists the eleven cities whose ratings were lower in 1987 than in 1977 and the four cities whose ratings improved during the same period. Significantly, more ratings were lowered than were raised. The seventeen big cities not shown in the table (excluding Washington, DC, which does not issue bonds) experienced no change in their bond ratings.

Table 6.3

Changes in Bond Ratings

	Bond Ratings	
	1977	1987
Cities with downgrade		
Houston	Aaa	Aa
Milwaukee	Aaa	Aa
San Francisco	Aaa	Aa1
Chicago	A1	Baa1
New Orleans	A	Baa
Boston	A	Baa1
Cleveland	A	Baa
Philadelphia	A	Baa
Pittsburgh	A	Baa1
St. Louis	A	Baa
Buffalo	Baa1	Baa
Cities with upgrade		
Phoenix	Aa	Aa1
San Diego	Aa	Aaa
Baltimore	A	A1
New York	Ba	Baa1

Source: Moody's Investors Services as reported in the International City Management Association, *Municipal Year Book* (Washington, DC: ICMA, 1978 and 1988).

Key to ratings: Aaa, Best Quality; Aa, high quality; A, upper-medium grade; Baa, medium grade; Ba, speculative; B, lacks characteristics of desirable investment; A1 and Baa1, strongest investment characteristics within the category.

Among the cities with declining ratios are three—Houston, Milwaukee, and San Francisco—that began the period with the highest rating and many cities that were listed in Table 6.2 as having budgetary problems. Notwithstanding the fact that bond ratings measure more than just financial condition, the large number of downgrades suggests a deterioration in the average financial condition of big cities.

Summary

The evidence on city financial condition is mixed. Although the average budgetary surplus of thirty-three big cities was slightly higher in the 1980s than in the 1970s, evidence of persistent skimpy surpluses suggests little improvement in the budgetary condition of many big cities. More-over, the fall in capital spending and the fact that more cities experienced downgrades than upgrades in bond ratings suggests that, contrary to the view of other observers, budgetary pressures persisted into the 1980s.

Tax Rates and Service Levels

Cities' more conservative financial management during the 1980s helped them cope with the fiscal pressures of the period and to avoid the severe financial crisis that New York City had faced in 1975 when it nearly defaulted on its loans. But their larger budgetary surpluses do not mean that big cities were more successfully meeting the public service needs of their residents. To the extent that balanced budgets were achieved by shifting to less desirable revenue sources, boosting tax rates, or cutting the quality of public services, city residents were worse off in the 1980s than in the 1970s. Hence, in this section, we look at the choices cities made during this period about taxes and service levels.

Revenue Mix

As was noted earlier, reductions in intergovernmental aid forced cities to rely more heavily on their own revenue sources. In addition, voter resistance to property taxes led many cities to increase their revenue from a variety of narrowly defined taxes and user fees. In 1977, the typical big city obtained 55 percent of its tax revenue from property taxes. By 1986, this share had fallen to 47.6 percent. Cities partially made up the slack by increased reliance on general sales, selective sales, and income taxes, and also a variety of narrowly defined taxes (see Table 6.1).

California cities, for example, maintained expenditures on basic ser-vices in the face of declining intergovernmental aid and property taxes by increasing utility users' taxes, transient lodging taxes, franchise fees and also by turning to nontax revenues from user charges.[10] Between 1977 and 1986, San Francisco increased the share of its own source revenues from user charges from 18 to 29 percent and Los Angeles increased its user charge share from 18 to 25 percent. However, not all big cities expanded reliance on user fees. Overall, eighteen of the thirty-three cities reported on did so while the other fifteen decreased their relative reliance on fees, perhaps because the fee schedules they had at the beginning of the period were not increased in line with the price level.[11] The shift to user charge financing in many cities may have provided incentives for more efficient spending decisions, but the general pattern of moving away from broad based taxes to narrowly defined taxes and fees probably increased the distortions of the tax system and certainly raised questions of tax fairness.

New nontax funds for cities also came from increased interest earnings and miscellaneous sources such as special assessments and sales of property. Thanks to high interest rates and more aggressive management of city assets, interest income increased from about 5½ percent to 10½ percent of own source revenues in the average big city during the period. Other miscellaneous revenues also increased by almost as much. To the extent that these miscellaneous funds come from sales of property, they are not revenue in the standard sense; instead they represent sales of assets and hence a diminution in the wealth of the government.

Tax Burdens

Tax burdens on city residents in the thirty-three big cities declined between 1977 and 1982, but then increased sufficiently after 1982 to produce a higher tax burden on city residents in 1986 than in 1977.[12] The decline in tax burdens in the early period largely reflects the effects of the tax revolt. Even though few big cities experienced the property tax rollbacks forced on California and Massachusetts cities, less-stringent tax limitations plus fear of taxpayer revolts apparently made city councils less willing to raise taxes than they might have been in a different tax environment.

After 1982, city officials became more willing to increase taxes. This increased willingness was partially a response to large cutbacks in federal aid under the Reagan administration, but may also reflect an attempt to maintain the quality of public services in the face of rising costs. Between 1982 and 1986, city tax burdens in the average big city rose by 19 percent for three broad based taxes and by 21 percent for all city taxes. Unless these tax increases were offset by comparable increases in local public services, they imply that city residents were worse off on average in 1986 than in 1982 or 1977.

Quality of Public Services

Because few good output measures are available, determining how the quality of public services provided to city residents has changed over time is a difficult task. Nonetheless, various pieces of evidence suggest that the quality of services received by city residents deteriorated between 1977 and 1986.

Consider, for example, safety from crime. Despite the measurement problems associated with the crime rates reported in the FBI's Uniform Crime Reports, changes in such rates undoubtedly provide useful information about changes over time in the safety of individual cities.[13] Between 1977 and 1982, the crime rate in the thirty-three big cities increased on average by 18 percent, with huge increases in Miami, Philadelphia, Seattle, and Washington, DC. During this five-year period, the reported crime rate fell in only four of the thirty-three. After 1982, the situation apparently improved with sixteen of the cities experiencing falling crime rates. Nonetheless, even in this more recent period, the average crime rate across all the cities in the study increased another 4.3 percent, yielding an average increase over the 1977–86 period of over 20 percent. This increase provides support for the view that residents of big cities experienced a lower level of public safety in the mid-1980s than in the mid-1970s.

The situation in urban schools has also become increasingly bleak over time. Cities have become the home for growing numbers of minority households who experience poverty at much higher rates than white households, and for large numbers of families headed by single parents with school-age children, who also are disproportionately poor. In addition, cities are increasingly bearing the burden of concentrations of extreme poverty. Thus, urban school systems have to cope not only with the learning handicaps associated with the poverty found in individual households, but also with the problems such as drug use, teenage parenting, violence, and unemployment associated with concentrations of extreme poverty. As a result, achievement levels are low and dropout rates high throughout urban school districts, but especially so in predominantly minority schools.[14]

Changes in city spending provide some indirect, but hard to interpret, information on city service levels. Table 6.4 summarizes average changes in per capita spending on all functions, on a set of functions that are common across most cities, and on public safety, with all numbers deflated by the national deflator for state and local government purchases. The table shows that per capita spending declined between 1977 and 1982 and then rebounded sharply after 1982. Over the entire period, real per capita spending increased by about 6 percent.

Table 6.4

**Per Capita Expenditures, 1977–86
(averages, thirty-two big cities)**

		Percent change		
	1986 (dollars)	1977–82	1982–86	1977–86
All functions (current account)	735	−1.8	9.7	5.6
Common functions	446	−2.9	9.6	6.3
Public safety	222	−5.0	12.7	6.6

Source: U.S. Department of Commerce, Bureau of the Census, *City Government Finances*, various years (Washington, DC: U.S. Government Printing Office).

Notes: See note 8 for list of cities. Washington, DC is excluded. Expenditures were deflated by the national deflator for state and local government purchases.

However, this 6 percent increase in real spending does not translate into a comparable increase in the quality of services. The main reason is that the state and local deflator does not include the effects on the cost of providing public services of changes in the environmental characteristics of the city. A city that has a harsher environment for providing public services, perhaps because a greater number of its residents are poor or because it has more commuters to serve, encounters higher costs of providing services than a city with a less harsh environment. Similarly, deterioration over time in the conditions under which cities provide services, caused, for example, by an increase in the incidence of poverty, boosts the cost of providing a given quality of public services. Ladd and Yinger have estimated that between 1977 and 1982 changes in city characteristics such as the poverty rate, per resident private employment in the city, and the composition of city economic activity boosted the costs of providing public safety in the average big city by over 35 percent and of other services by about 6 percent.[15] Even if we assume unrealistically that costs remained constant after 1982, the spending rebound in the recent period falls far short of what would have been needed to offset the service declines of the previous five years. Hence, despite the small increase in real spending between 1977 and 1986, service levels in big cities appear to be lower in 1986 than they were in the mid-1970s.

Fiscal Health

The rise in tax burdens and the fall in service quality reflect a basic deterioration over time in the ability of big cities to provide adequate public services at reasonable tax rates, that is, in their fiscal health. A city has poor fiscal health if its capacity to generate revenue is small relative to its expenditure needs.

The concept of expenditure need recognizes that some cities face higher costs of providing a given package of public services than others because of city characteristics such as population density or the incidence of poverty that are outside the control of city officials. Revenue-raising capacity represents the revenue a city could generate by imposing a standard tax burden expressed as a percentage of income on its residents augmented by its ability to export tax burdens to nonresidents. A city in poor fiscal health would have to impose above-average tax rates to provide a standard package of services or must accept below-average service levels if it chooses to impose average tax rates. A city in strong fiscal health, in contrast, has substantial capacity to generate revenue relative to its expenditure need and can achieve standard service levels at below-average tax rates.

Over time two sets of factors affect the fiscal health of cities. The first set includes economic and social factors, such as the income of city residents, the poverty rate, and the suburbanization of employment that affect either a city's ability to raise revenue or its cost of providing a given quality of public services or both. The second set includes the fiscal institutions within which the city operates. For example a city that has access to broad based taxes other than the property tax, receives a lot of state aid, or provides a limited array of public services will have stronger fiscal health, all other factors held constant, than will a city whose power to tax is restricted to the property tax, that receives minimal state aid, and that has extensive service responsibilities.

Standardized Fiscal Health

In their comprehensive study of seventy major central cities, Ladd and Yinger document a significant deterioration between 1972 and 1982 in the fiscal health of U.S. central cities, and more specifically America's biggest cities.[16] Table 6.5 summarizes their results for their concept of standardized fiscal health, the calculation of which is based on the

Table 6.5

Standardized Fiscal Health in 1982 (seventy central cities)

	Number of cities	Revenue-raising capacity	Standardized expenditure need	Capacity minus need	Fiscal health index
Illustrative cities					
Atlanta	1	$505	$640	$(136)	−26.9%
Baltimore	1	331	483	152	−45.7
Boston	1	501	561	59	−11.9
Detroit	1	341	654	(313)	−91.9
Denver	1	532	505	27	5.0
Washington, DC	1	624	535	89	14.3
All cities in sample					
Average	70	$425	$458	$(33)	−10.9%
Standard deviation	70	80	109	128	32.2
Maximum	70	649	737	290	47.2
Minimum	70	286	243	(386)	−109.7
Cities grouped by population (in thousands)					
Less than 100	6	$457	$384	$ 74	16.4%
100–250	19	473	421	52	9.1
250–500	26	420	473	(53)	−13.5
500–1,000	14	385	466	(80)	−22.9
Greater than 1,000	5	341	586	(245)	−72.8

Source: Helen F. Ladd and John Yinger, *America's Ailing Cities: Fiscal Health and the Design of Urban Policy* (Baltimore, MD: Johns Hopkins University Press, 1989), Tables 5.1 and 5.2.

Note: See note 16 for description of the seventy cities.

assumption that each city operates within the same standardized set of fiscal institutions. *Revenue-raising capacity* indicates the amount of revenue that a city could generate from three broad-based taxes—property, general sales, and earnings—at a standard tax burden on its residents. *Standardized expenditure need* indicates the amount the city would have to spend to provide a standard set of public services, given the effects of its socioeconomic characteristics, such as its poverty rate, on the costs of providing those services. *Standardized fiscal health* is defined as each city's revenue-raising capacity minus its expenditure need expressed as a percentage of capacity. Because of the assumption of uniform fiscal institutions, differences across cities and over time in standardized fiscal health reflect economic and social factors alone.

The top panel of the table reports indexes of standardized fiscal health in 1982 and its components for six illustrative big cities and averages for seventy central cities grouped by size of city. The indexes are constructed using a 1972 baseline service level, defined as the quality of services that the average city could provide at a standard tax burden on city residents in 1972. A positive fiscal health index, such as those for Denver or Washington, implies that the city's revenue-raising capacity was greater than its expenditure need and indicates that the city's fiscal health in 1982 exceeded that of the average major central city in 1972. The specific value (5 percent for Denver and 14 percent for Washington) indicates the percentage of its revenue the city would have had left over for increases in service quality or for tax cuts in 1982 after it had provided the 1972 average service quality at the standard tax burden.

A negative fiscal health index, such as those for Atlanta, Baltimore, Boston, and Detroit, implies that a city's 1982 capacity was less than its expenditure need and indicates that the city's fiscal health was weaker in 1982 than that of the average major central city in 1972. For example, Detroit's fiscal health index of –92 indicates that it had a standardized expenditure need that was almost twice as high as its standardized revenue-raising capacity. Detroit would have had to receive a 92 percent boost in its revenue-raising capacity from outside sources to be able to provide services of the quality that the average city could provide out of its own broad-based revenue sources in 1972.

The average standardized fiscal health of the cities in the Ladd-Yinger study was –11 percent in 1982. This figure means that the typical central city would have needed a boost in revenues of 11 percent from outside sources in 1982 to provide the 1972 baseline service level at the standard

standard tax burden. In other words, economic and social forces significantly weakened the fiscal health of the typical city during the period.

Cities with population over 250,000 fared the worst. The negative average index in the three largest size categories of cities indicates that the standardized fiscal health of America's biggest cities was significantly poorer than that of smaller cities. In contrast to the −11 percent index for all seventy cities, cities in the three largest size categories had average indexes of −14, −23, and −73 percent.

Actual Fiscal Health

Dropping the assumption that cities operate within a uniform set of fiscal institutions leads, in the Ladd-Yinger terminology, to a city's actual fiscal health. Actual fiscal health measures the balance between a city's actual expenditure need (its need adjusted for its service responsibilities) and its restricted revenue-raising capacity (its capacity restricted by the taxes it is empowered to use, adjusted for capacity used up by overlying jurisdictions, and augmented by state aid). Standardized to a 1972 average service level, actual fiscal health measures a city's ability to provide the 1972 baseline service level at a standard tax burden on city residents, given the fiscal institutions within which the city operates.

Table 6.6 provides information on 1982 levels and 1972–82 changes in actual fiscal health for cities grouped by population.[17] The measures of actual fiscal health are interpreted analogously to those of standardized fiscal health. In particular, the −4.9 percent in the first cell of column 2 means that the average city in 1982 would need additional resources equal to almost 5 percent of its revenue-raising capacity to provide the 1972 baseline service level at the standard tax burden on city residents. This negative number implies that the typical city was worse off in 1982 than in 1972. However, comparing the 4.9 percent decline in average actual health with the 10.9 percent average decline in standardized health from Table 6.5 indicates that changes in fiscal institutions have helped offset some of the adverse effects of economic and social factors; in other words, state actions such as authorizing use of additional taxes, taking over welfare services, or giving more aid mitigated some, but not all, of the adverse fiscal effects of economic and social trends that buffeted American cities during the 1970s.

Even after accounting for the beneficial effects of state fiscal institutions, the 1982 average fiscal health of cities in the three largest size

Table 6.6

Actual Fiscal Health
(averages by category of city, seventy central cities)

	Number of cities	Actual fiscal health	Change in actual fiscal health (percentage point)
Average[a]	70	−4.9	−4.9
Cities grouped by population (in thousands)			
Less than 100	6	14.6	7.0
100–250	19	6.4	−9.2
250–500	26	−9.0	−4.4
500–1,000	14	−5.5	−4.6[b]
Greater than 1,000	5	−48.1	−20.8

Source: Helen F. Ladd and John M. Yinger, *America's Ailing Cities: Fiscal Health and the Design of Urban Policy* (Baltimore, MD: Johns Hopkins University Press, 1989), Tables 9.2 and 9.3.

[a]See note 16 for description of the sample of cities.

[b]Figure excludes Cincinnati because of a possible data problem with the 1972 figure for that city.

categories was negative. The largest cities, for example, would have needed additional revenues equal to 48 percent of their revenue-raising capacity to provide the 1972 baseline service level at the standard tax burden on city residents. This finding contrasts with a positive average fiscal health of 14.6 percent for cities with less than 100,000 people. In contrast to the larger cities, these smaller cities not only could raise sufficient revenues at the standard tax burden to provide the 1972 baseline service level, but they would also have had revenues left over to improve services or to reduce tax burdens.

By construction, the average 1972–82 change for all seventy cities is the same as the average index for 1982. Column 3 shows that the largest cities experienced the greatest decline in capacity relative to needs; on average their actual fiscal health declined by almost twenty-one percentage points during the decade. In general, no clear pattern of decline emerges across cities grouped by population size. The main point is simply that, on average, cities in all the size categories over 100,000 experienced declining actual fiscal health during the 1972–82 decade.

Recent Trends

Because 1982 was a recession year, one might wonder whether the cities' poor fiscal health in that year reflects a short term cyclical downturn rather than the effects of longer term trends. However, this cyclical interpretation of the 1982 figures is not consistent with the trends since 1982 in three key contributors to city fiscal health: the income of city residents, central city poverty rates, and support from state governments.

With respect to the major determinant of the revenue-raising capacity of a city, namely the income of city residents, cities fared less well during the 1981–85 period than during the 1977–81 period.[18] During the four years ending in 1985, real resident income declined in fifteen of the thirty-three big cities listed in note 8, while the average big city experienced only a 0.6 percent increase. During the previous four-year period, resident income declined in ten cities and the average city experienced a 1.7 percent increase. Over the entire period, real income declined in two out of five of the thirty-three big cities. To be sure, the income situation brightened in some cities. Notable examples are Boston, where real income grew by 21 percent during the eight-year period, Atlanta where income grew by 7.5 percent in the recent period, after declining in the earlier period, and Portland, Oregon, where resident income partially recovered in the recent period from its dramatic decline in the earlier period. Nonetheless, many U.S. cities experienced declining real income during the 1980s and this trend is likely to continue into the future.

The aggregate incidence of poverty in all central cities was substantially higher in 1986 than in 1970. Although the 1986 rate of 18 percent fell below the 1982 peak of 19.9 percent, the trends provide little reason for optimism; the poverty rate in U.S. central cities has exceeded the U.S. average by about a third for each of the past several years. With no national leadership to reduce poverty, the rate of poverty in the nation's big cities and the costs associated with that poverty of providing public services are likely to remain high. Cities will continue to be called upon to provide social services for the poor, shelters for the homeless, and additional police services to deal with the social problems that arise when there are concentrations of extreme poverty.

Moreover, fiscal pressures at the state level have kept the states from doing much to help their cities in the mid-1980s. How much the states have assisted their cities since 1982 is difficult to determine because, as discussed above, state assistance encompasses more than just the provision of state aid; it also includes state assumption of city expenditure responsibilities and authorization to use additional broad-based taxes. If we focus just on state aid, however, the one component of the assistance package for which recent information is available, we find no evidence of increased state support for big central cities in recent years. Indeed, between 1982 and 1986, average state aid to thirty-two of the big cities (excluding Washington, DC) remained constant at 19 percent of city general expenditures; aid as a percent of spending went down in seventeen cities and up in fifteen cities. Moreover, no clear pattern emerges across cities grouped by their 1982 fiscal health. This trend since 1982 contrasts with the trend before 1982 when state aid increased from under 16 percent to 19 percent of city spending.

Summary and Conclusion

The Ladd-Yinger measures of the underlying or structural fiscal health of U.S. cities indicate a significant deterioration over time. They imply that social and economic trends made it more difficult for many big cities in 1982 than in 1972 to provide a standard package of public services at reasonable tax burdens on their residents. Although state governments offset some of the adverse effects of these trends, state assistance was not large enough to keep the fiscal health of the big cities from deteriorating. Moreover, recent trends in the income of city residents, poverty rates, and state aid suggest that the trends identified by Ladd and Yinger have continued into more recent years.

   Overall, the fiscal outlook for many of America's big cities is not rosy. Although more conservative financial management has helped them to avoid the financial problems faced by New York City in 1975, the new 1980s brand of federalism has not been kind to them. Through no fault of their own, many big cities are experiencing declining fiscal health. This trend is likely to continue and may be exacerbated by the effects of the Tax Reform Act of 1986. During the 1970s, federal aid to cities played an important role in helping cities provide adequate public services at reasonable tax rates. But much of that assistance is no longer forthcoming. Without additional injections of either federal aid or state assistance to their cities, residents in many big cities will continue to experience significant deterioration in the quality of public services or higher tax burdens or both.

Notes

1. George E. Peterson, "Finance," in W. Gorham and N. Glazer, eds., 35, *The Urban Predicament* (Washington, DC: Urban Institute Press, 1976).

2. Ibid., Table 2, p. 41.

3. For an insightful discussion of the forces that led to the rise and fall of federal aid to urban areas, see Robert Reischauer, "The Rise and Fall of National Urban Policy: The Fiscal Dimension," in Marshall Kaplan and Franklin James, eds., *The Future of National Urban Policy* (Durham, NC: Duke University Press, forthcoming).

4. The federal programs of importance to urban local governments and the percentage change in their budget authority between 1980 and 1987 include Wastewater Treatment Construction (–32.2), Urban Mass Transportation (–27.4), Urban and Secondary Roads (–22.5), Community Development Block Grants (–20.0), Urban Development Action Grants (–66.7), Housing Subsidy Programs (–56.7), Training and Employment (–46.0), Compensatory Education (–10.3), and General Revenue Sharing (–100). Together the budget authority for these programs declined from $45.3 billion in 1980 to $24.1 billion in 1987. During this same period budget authority for all other grants increased from $59.7 billion to $87.6 billion. Excluding AFDC and Medicaid, budget authority for all other grants increased from $37.6 billion to $49.5 billion or by 31.8 percent. Source: Peggy L. Cuciti, "A Non-Urban Policy: Recent Policy Shifts Affecting Cities," in Marshall Kaplan and Franklin James, eds., *The Future of National Urban Policy* (Durham, NC: Duke University Press, forthcoming), Table 3.

5. For a discussion of the impacts of the TRA on the municipal bond market, see John Peterson, "Examining the Impacts of the 1986 Tax Reform Act on the Municipal Securities Market," *National Tax Journal* 40, 3 (September 1987), 393–402 and for its initial impacts on city finances, see Michael A. Pagano, "The Effects of the 1986 Tax Reform Act on City Finances: An Appraisal of Year One" (research report of the National League of Cities, Washington, DC, 1987).

6. See Edward M. Gramlich, "The Deductibility of State and Local Taxes," *National Tax Journal* 38, 4 (December 1985), 447–465; Roy Bahl, "Urban Government Finance and Federal Income Tax Reform," *National Tax Journal* 40 (March 1987), 1–18; Paul Courant and Daniel Rubinfeld, "Tax Reform: Implications for the State-Local Public Sector," *Journal of Economic Perspectives* (Summer 1987), 87–100; and Howard Chernick and Andrew Reschovsky, "The Effect of Federal Tax Reform on State Fiscal Systems: Some Preliminary Evidence," paper prepared for the session on Federal, State, and Local Relations of the American Economic Association, December 1988.

7. Philip M. Dearborn, "Fiscal Conditions in Large American Cities, 1971–1984," in Michael M.G. McGeary and Lawrence Lynn, eds., 281, *Urban Change and Poverty* (Washington, DC: National Academy Press, 1988).

8. The data for these comparisons come primarily from U.S. Department of Commerce, Bureau of the Census, *City Government Finances* (Washington, DC: USGPO, various years). The thirty-three cities are Atlanta, Baltimore, Boston, Buffalo, Chicago, Cincinnati, Cleveland, Columbus, Dallas, Denver, Detroit, Houston, Indianapolis, Jacksonville, Kansas City, Los Angeles, Memphis, Miami, Milwaukee, Minneapolis, New Orleans, New York, Philadelphia, Phoenix, Pittsburgh,

Portland, St. Louis, San Antonio, San Diego, San Francisco, San Jose, Seattle, and Washington, DC

9. For each city, surpluses (or deficits) are measured as the difference between annual current account expenditures (which include debt service and contributions to city retirement systems, but exclude capital outlays) and revenues expressed as a percentage of expenditures. Revenues exclude the primary source of financing for capital projects, namely bond proceeds. However, because the revenue measure includes some intergovernmental aid for capital projects and possibly some own-source revenues used for capital projects, it represents more than revenue for current expenditure. This fact should lead to larger measured surpluses (or smaller deficits) than would occur if current account revenues were correctly measured.

10. For a detailed analysis, see Gary Reid, "How Cities in California Have Responded to Fiscal Pressures Since Proposition 13," *Public Budgeting and Finance* 8, 1 (Spring 1988), 20–37.

11. Another possible explanation is that some cities may have set up special authorities, such as the water and sewer commission in Boston, to provide services financed more heavily by user charges. The resulting increased reliance on user charges would not show up in the city's general purpose revenues.

12. Measuring tax burdens on city residents is complicated because some of a city's taxes are exported to nonresidents, and cities differ in the range of public services for which they are responsible and hence in the taxes required to meet those responsibilities. To make them comparable across cities with different economic and fiscal structures, the tax burdens referred to in the text were calculated as a city's tax revenues divided by its restricted revenue-raising capacity. See below for further discussion of restricted capacity, and for more detail on the calculation and interpretation of big city tax burdens see Helen F. Ladd, "Big City Finances" (paper to be published under the auspices of the Taubman Center for State and Local Government, Kennedy School of Government, Harvard University).

13. Criticisms of the *Uniform Crime Reports* include the fact that the crime index includes only those crimes known to the police, that guidelines for reporting crimes may vary from one police department to another, that police officers exercise some discretion in what they report, that the index weights different crimes equally, and that rates are not expressed relative to the populations that could be exposed to that crime. See, for example, Albert J. Reiss, Jr., "Assessing the Current Crime Wave," in Barbara McLennan, ed., 23–44, *Crime in Urban Society* (New York: Dunellen, 1970).

14. For a detailed discussion of the problems of urban education, see Frank Newman, Robert Palaich, and Rona Wilensky, "Re-engaging State and Federal Policymakers in the Problems of Urban Education," in Marshall Kaplan and Franklin Jones, eds., *The Future of National Urban Policy* (Durham, NC: Duke University Press, forthcoming).

15. These estimates of cost indexes are based on a regression model of city expenditures that isolates the impact on city expenditures of city characteristics that are outside the control of local officials. For a full discussion of the underlying theory and measurement of these cost indexes, see Helen F. Ladd and John Yinger, *America's Ailing Cities: Fiscal Health and the Design of Urban Policy* (Baltimore: Johns Hopkins University Press, 1989), chapter 4.

16. The sample of seventy cities is a subset of the eighty-six major American central cities where major central cities are defined as cities with population over

300,000 in either 1970 or 1980 or smaller cities that served as central cities in one of the nation's fifty largest metropolitan areas in either 1970 or 1980. The sample of seventy cities represents all cities other than Washington, DC for which complete data were available. For the list of cities, see Helen F. Ladd and John Yinger, *America's Ailing Cities*, Table 1.1, p. 11.

17. Breakdowns by revenue-raising capacity and expenditure need are not presented because the components of fiscal institutions are too intertwined to permit a meaningful interpretation of the capacity and need sides of actual fiscal health. For example, a city that has low service responsibilities is likely to have more of its local revenue-raising capacity used up by overlying jurisdictions and consequently to have a smaller revenue-raising capacity than a city with a larger, wider range of responsibilities. In addition, the city may well receive less state aid. Hence, the observation that a city has low actual expenditure needs is not meaningful without reference to its revenue-raising capacity; what matters is the balance between the two, as measured by actual fiscal health.

18. The dividing year is 1981 because the Ladd-Yinger capacity measures for 1982 are based on 1981 income; the income of city residents is not available for even years.

The Economics of Fiscal Federalism and Its Reform

EDWARD M. GRAMLICH

The United States has always had one of the best-developed systems of fiscal federalism in the world. The fifty states have a large degree of autonomy from the national government: there are 75,000 local governments and special taxing districts that have a large degree of autonomy from both the national government and their state government. More than 3 percent of GNP is devoted to grants and tax expenditures paid by the national government for the benefit of states and localities, and another 3 percent devoted to grants paid by states to localities. State government direct (nongrant) spending accounts for 6 percent of GNP and local government spending for another 8 percent.

It should not be surprising that various aspects of this extensive system of fiscal relations have been examined thoroughly and often. Pages of several leading journals have been full of articles about federalism for decades. While it is impossible to distill an exact consensus out of this extensive literature, there is a broad consensus on a few important features concerning how a system of fiscal relationships between governments should be organized. In this paper I summarize that consensus, and then attempt the more interesting job of comparing the existing U.S. system to this normative ideal. The two match up surprisingly well, but as might be expected, there are still discrepancies—discrepancies that are a good place to look in designing policy reform proposals.

Divisions of Responsibility: A Normative Model

The paper begins by comparing actual divisions of responsibility among governments for spending programs with the responsibilities that might be predicted by normative theoretical considerations. I divide spending into programs that are done for collective consumption motives, those that redistribute income, and those that provide social insurance. For each, the actual division of responsibility is compared to the theoretical ideal. Then I repeat the exercise on the tax side of the budget and for intergovernmental grants and tax subsidies. The instances turned up by this tour, where the present system does not conform well to the theoretical ideal, inspire a few suggested reforms to remedy the defects. Each of the suggested reforms should improve economic efficiency and equity, and the whole package together would make a sizable dent in the federal budget deficit.

Spending

The logic behind any division of functional responsibilities among governments follows directly from the logic that rationalizes government intervention in a market economy in the first place. Governments are collective organizations that can do certain things more efficiently than private individuals: protect rights, enforce laws and contracts, provide public goods, alter the distribution of income, and provide insurance against privately uninsurable risks. The last three in particular have been the focus of economists in their writing about government intervention in market economies, and I now extend the same logic to deal with federalism questions.

Public Goods

The public goods rationale for intervening in a market economy is that certain goods have the physical property that it is difficult or costly to exclude consumers from consumption. Examples are lighthouses, defense goods, public parks, and streets, all of which provide benefits to those who do not pay for the good along with benefits to those who do pay. Given this physical property, it is difficult or costly for the provider of these goods to sell services to pay for them; and difficult or impossible for any one consumer to charge others for the external benefits yielded by her or his own consumption. Hence when people consume such goods individually, there will be suboptimal consumption levels because the individual consumers will not take into account the benefits of all others who consume automatically by virtue of the individual's consumption. The remedy is to provide the goods collectively, working out some political arrangements to vote on and pay for the goods jointly.

This reasoning is normally used to justify public intervention in a market economy, but it also provides a good platform from which to think about the division of functional responsibilities among governments. Beginning with any one individual, the advantage of organizing collectively, or adding individuals to the decision-making unit, is that others reap external benefits from the consumption activity. Hence the group gets closer to the social optimum level of consumption if more individuals are brought into the collective decision-making unit: the external benefits of consumption by one party are made internal.

On the other side, the disadvantage of adding people to the collective process is that at some point strong differences in tastes are likely to emerge. At some point the external benefits for a particular consumption item begin to decrease. Since the relatively unwilling consumers are forced to pay some share of the cost of the good, they will not obtain their desired amount unless they are taxed according to their marginal willingness to pay, a difficult requirement in the real world. This leads to rising distortionary costs as people are added to the decision-making unit.

While it may be difficult to apply in practice, this reasoning leads to a proposition about the optimally sized jurisdiction for the provision of any public good. A jurisdiction has reached this optimal size when the marginal advantage of adding people and reducing externalities equals the marginal disadvantage of adding people and increasing distortionary losses from taste differences.[1] If there is a public good that makes nobody outside the city better off—a public park in an area inaccessible to outsiders—the good should be provided by the city, because there are no externalities to be internalized in adding others to the political unit, but there is still a rising distortionary cost. If on the other hand there is a good from which all individuals in the country benefit, such as national defense and foreign aid, the good should be provided by the national government because there is a gain from internalizing the externalities, and minimal cost in forcing various consumers to consume the same amount.

Income Distribution

A second problem requiring public intervention in a market economy involves the distribution of income. A market economy distributes income according to the marginal product of labor and capital owned, yielding what could be wide extremes in income between rich and poor. Public taxes and transfers are necessary to limit this variance in outcomes.

There is a federalism dimension to income distribution as well. If the jurisdiction for which redistribution is being carried out is a small one, rich people who would be taxed have an easy escape—they can leave the community. By contrast, poor people have an incentive to enter the community to gain from the redistribution, hence raising the number of poor people and the cost of redistribution for the remaining taxpayers. It follows that redistribution over a wide area such as a nation, where both emigration and immigration are quite costly, is more efficient than redistribution over a narrow area where emigration and immigration are relatively cheap.[2]

Social Insurance

A third rationale for government intervention in the private market involves social insurance. People desire many types of insurance against social risks: insurance against old age poverty, catastrophic medical disability, long term unemployment. Since the costs of providing this type of insurance could be large, are quite uncertain, are realized in the long run, and are heavily concentrated in particular geographic areas, private insurers have been reluctant to provide it. Backed up by the ultimate power to tax, governments have provided this insurance, often forcing private citizens to join the scheme and contribute to costs.

Although social insurance schemes could in principle be provided by any level of government, many of the risk-pooling considerations that argue for them in the first place argue for national schemes. Most social insurance schemes work over the life cycle—workers pay in when working, and receive benefits when they are retired, in need of medical care, unemployed, or disabled. The United States is a country with a great degree of mobility across state borders, and many claimants on the social insurance fund will be living in a different state when time comes to collect benefits. It would not be impossible to work out a system of state payments to keep track of people moving from state to state, but it is generally cheaper just to assign people a national social security number and finance national benefits for people wherever they are. National trust funds for social insurance programs are neither inevitable nor unavoidable, but they are probably more efficient than state trust funds when the population is mobile.

Actual Budgets

Although the propositions outlined in the previous section are vague and often hard to apply, the actual division of responsibilities for spending programs among governments conforms reasonably well to the theoretical standards. Table 7.1 gives a breakdown of what is called direct spending at various levels of government for 1985. Direct spending is total spending less interest payments less grants to other governments. Interest payments are excluded because they merely reflect the fiscal history of the respective governments; grants, so that the government actually running the program gets credit for it, even if the spending is partly financed by a grant from some other government. The table also designates whether each type of spending program is fundamentally a public goods program (P), a redistribution program (R), or a social insurance program (S). For these purposes education is considered a public good, even though there are certain ways in which education does not satisfy the requirements of being a public good (more consumers can use a bridge without much cost; the same cannot be said of a classroom or a college).

The table shows that relatively few public goods are operated by the national government. The only ones are those with a clear national span of benefits such as national defense, foreign aid, and veterans' benefits, which are properly thought of as an adjunct to national defense—and all social insurance programs are operated by the national government. The public goods programs operated by state governments—highways and health and hospitals—are those that must be planned regionally and in effect have a geographic span of benefits that exceeds local areas. The remaining public goods are operated locally.

But two aspects of the actual division of spending responsibility are harder to justify from a normative point of view. First, the redistribution programs at all levels of government are mixed in a way that no one could justify very convincingly. Some—agricultural subsidies and food stamps—are financed and operated at the national level; some—welfare and Medicaid—are partly financed by federal grants but actually run by states or localities. One of the reform proposals I will make below involves sorting these welfare responsibilities out more cleanly.

The second area where the actual responsibility is hard to justify involves higher education. Higher education is mainly financed by grants or tuition reductions from state governments to students. It is

Table 7.1

Direct Expenditures of Various Levels of Government, 1985

Item	Type	Amount in billions of current dollars	Percent of GNP
National		754.7	18.8
National defense	P	259.0	6.5
Social Security	S	166.8	4.2
Medicare	S	72.0	1.8
Agricultural subsidies	R	29.8	0.7
Veterans' benefits	P	28.8	0.7
Disability insurance	S	26.3	0.7
Welfare (food stamps)	R	21.9	0.5
Unemployment insurance	S	15.9	0.4
Foreign aid	P	14.3	0.4
Other		119.9	3.0
State		236.3	5.9
Higher education	P	41.0	1.0
Medical care (Medicaid)	R	40.5	1.0
Highways	P	26.4	0.7
Health and hospitals	P	25.2	0.6
Welfare	R	23.3	0.6
Other		79.9	2.0
Local		310.6	7.7
Elementary, secondary education	P	142.0	3.5
Police and fire	P	32.3	0.8
Health and hospitals	P	26.9	0.7
Welfare	R	17.5	0.4
Highways	P	16.9	0.4
Sewage and sanitation	P	9.5	0.2
Other		65.5	1.6

Source: David J. Levin and Donald C. Peters, ''Receipts and Expenditures of State Governments and of Local Governments: Revised and Updated Estimates, 1983–1986,'' *Survey of Current Business* 67 (November 87), 29–35.

not clear why the subsidy should be a grant, and the donor the state government. Students recapture a reasonable share of their education expenses in the form of higher postgraduate incomes, and it is not clear why taxpayers at large should provide grants, as opposed to loans. Moreover, it is not clear why these taxpayers should be at the state level, as opposed to some other level of government. These questions lead to a proposal for an alternative approach to the financing of higher education. Under this alternative, students would receive loans for their education, to be repaid later either on a present value basis or on an income related basis. With this latter arrangement, many of the advantages of having national trust funds would come into play, and it would be logical to move this credit-type subsidy for higher education up to the national level.

Taxation

On the tax side, the lessons are much the same as on the spending side. Taxes with a high redistributional content—those that take from the rich and give to the poor—should generally be imposed over a large jurisdiction from which emigration and immigration are costly. If not, the rich can leave and go to where they are not taxed so heavily. Taxes imposed by localities should look more like benefit charges, where the consumers that actually benefit from the public goods pay the cost. This insures a close correspondence of actual and desired spending for citizens of local governments. And social insurance fees should be assessed at the same level of government as the trust fund that finances their benefits.

The actual distribution of taxes in 1985 by the three levels of government is shown in Table 7.2. In line with the theoretical prediction, income and corporate taxes are relied on much more heavily by the national government. The income taxes that are imposed at the state level are generally of the flat-rate variety, generally not entailing much redistribution. There are some state corporate taxes, but since not all states impose such taxes, firms tend to flee high corporate tax states, and the corporate tax rates in those states that still have such taxes seem destined to remain at very low levels.

Sales taxes, which entail very little redistribution, and property taxes, which are probably the closest to benefit charges, are not used at all at the national level, but only at the state and local level. Social insurance charges for the national trust fund benefits—for old age pensions, Medicare, disability, and unemployment—are imposed entirely at the national level. The small social insurance fees at the state and local level are for pension plans for the employees of these governments, which naturally would be operated by the governments for which the employees worked.

Table 7.2

Taxes of Various Levels of Government, 1985

Item	Amount in billions of current dollars	Percent of GNP
National	788.7	19.7
Income	339.3	8.5
Corporate	58.5	1.5
Social insurance	310.9	7.8
Excise	34.6	0.9
Customs	12.2	0.3
Other	33.2	0.8
State	283.5	7.1
Income	66.1	1.6
Corporate	18.9	0.5
Social insurance	32.0	0.8
Sales	109.0	2.7
Other	57.5	1.4
Local	196.4	4.9
Social insurance	10.1	0.3
Sales	21.9	0.5
Property	103.4	2.6
Other	61.0	1.5

Source: See Table 7.1.

Grants and Subsidies

The role of grants and subsidies in a federal system is to take care of those instances where jurisdictions and spending responsibilities cannot be perfectly matched. Even if a public service is provided by the optimally sized jurisdiction, there will be some benefit spillovers—some benefits realized by outsiders. These present a rationale for categorical grants from the national government to states and localities. Even if there is a national income redistribution plan, there will be some regional income differences and these could lead to differential abilities to support public services. They present a rationale for noncategorical assistance from the national government to states and localities.

Categorical Grants

The basic rationale for categorical grants is benefit spillovers. Suppose that a jurisdiction's public spending generates some benefits to those living outside the jurisdiction. Just as individuals underconsume public goods when others benefit but do not pay, so also the jurisdiction will underconsume public goods unless the externalities can be internalized. One way of internalizing these externalities is for those outside the jurisdiction to bribe those inside to consume more.[3] But if there are lots of spending programs with externalities affecting lots of governments, the requisite system of bribes may be quite costly to work out. Further, there is no theoretical reason why the bargains among governments will ultimately be made: the various parties may simply hold out for better deals. In the end it is probably simpler for the national government just to provide price subsidies to encourage greater consumption of whatever public service it is that generates the externalities. These price subsidies, rebates of a certain share of the cost of certain public expenditures, are known as categorical grants.

To see how the system works, refer to Figure 7.1. Suppose the demand for a public service within a community is given by D_0 and the total demand including externalities is given by D_1. If the community faces a price, say equal to the marginal cost, of P, it will consume at quantity Q_0. The social optimum level of consumption including the externalities is Q^*. This level of consumption can be achieved by what is known as an open-ended categorical grant equal to m^* of the cost of this public service. The subsidy lowers the price to $P(1-m^*)$, the community goes to Q^*, and everybody lives happily ever after.

The national government has an extensive system of categorical grants, shown in Table 7.3 as $42.3 billion in 1987, 1 percent of GNP. About half of these grants are in areas where there would seem to be benefit spillovers, particularly transportation and sewage treatment. But even for these grants, the correspondence between the actual system and the theoretical ideal breaks down for two reasons:

- The grant matching ratios, shown in the right column, are very high, much higher than would be rationalized by benefit spillovers.
- Perhaps because of this, the grants are not open-ended.

The upshot of these two drawbacks can be seen from Figure 7.1. The

Figure 7.1. **The Inefficiency of Categorical Grants**

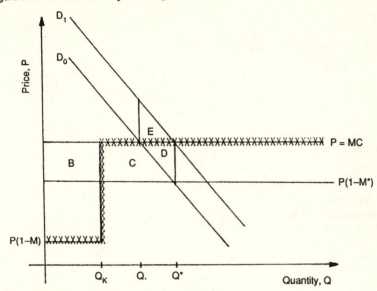

Notes: M is actual matching rate, M* is efficient rate yielding Q*.
xxxx is effective price schedule.
Converting inefficient to efficient grants yields the following gains and losses:
 Federal taxpayers gain area (A–C–D)
 State citizens gain area (C–A)
 Outsiders gain area (D+E)
 Net gain is area E

ideal price structure from an efficiency standpoint is a price line that is flat at P(1–m*). The actual price line features highly favorable national matching provisions out to the grant limit amount, Q_K, but then no more matching. The price line reverts to P, the community consumes Q_0, and we have the ironic result that because the matching rate was too favorable, the amount had to be limited, and the limited categorical grant does not encourage any added spending.

Were grants made efficient by switching to the flat price line at P(1–m*), national taxpayers would gain area (A–C–D). State citizens would gain area (C–A) and outsiders would gain area (E+D). The net gain of all together, known as the Kaldor-Hicks gain, is area E, that reflects the present-day loss of the underconsumption. Converting grants in this way thus improves economic efficiency, and it will reduce the federal budget deficit if area (A–C–D) is positive. I propose, below, to convert grants in this manner.

Table 7.3

Limited Federal Categorical Grants, 1987

Type	Amount in billions of current dollars	Matching rate (%)
Highways	12.3	83
Compensatory education	3.1	100
Employment and training	2.9	94
Sewage treatment	2.6	55
Mass transit	2.0	80
Human services	1.9	83
Public housing	1.9	100
Unemployment trust fund	1.6	100
Food donations	1.4	100
Rehabilitation services	1.3	83
Handicapped	1.2	99
Vocational education	1.0	58
Airports	0.9	80
Others	8.2	nc
Total	42.3	81

Source: Unpublished Office of Management and Budget data.

Noncategorical Grants

The rationale for categorical grants is based on the properties of the public good or service—whether there are external benefits. The rationale for noncategorical grants, given to augment the spendable resources of the recipient community without regard for what the community does with the grants, is based on the properties of the recipient government. If this government presides over a poor jurisdiction, with below-average income that can be taxed to provide public goods, its "tax price" for public services is higher than average and it will have subpar consumption levels of the public service. This would present no particular problem unless the public service in question were something like education. In that case the local financing of the public service in effect perpetuates the income disparity: poor communities have high tax prices for education, they stay poor, their tax price stays high, and so forth.

munity, either by a categorical or a noncategorical grant. The other half of the federal grants shown in Table 7.3—those for compensatory education, employment and training, human services, handicapped and vocational education—have this rationale. Even more significant are what are known as "power equalization" grants from state governments to local governments. These power equalization grants in effect try to equalize education spending across states by differential price reductions. Approximately 2 percent of GNP is devoted to education grants from states to localities, though it is hard to know how much equalization of tax prices is implicit in these grants without much more detailed analysis. The recently killed federal general revenue sharing program could also be rationalized along these lines, though the distribution of funds in that program was not particularly focused on poor districts.

There would be grounds for a policy reform in this area, but the case is a good deal weaker than in other areas because the states are already assuming responsibility for district power equalization. Any new federal initiatives, along the lines of upgraded compensatory education programs, risk causing reductions in such programs at the state level, and hence merely transferring resources from federal to state taxpayers. Moreover, it is hard to work out the details of the program because there are such wide differences in functional responsibilities and tax prices across states. In Hawaii, for example, the state government runs the schools—how would the national government work out a grant that treats Honolulu and some equally sized city with responsibility for its own schools even handedly? For this reason no federal power equalization scheme will be suggested below, though a case for it could certainly be made.

Tax Subsidies

There are two main tax subsidies that flow from the federal government to states and localities:

  • State and local income and property taxes are now deductible on the federal income tax, permitting some state taxpayers to recover some of their state and local taxes.
  • State and local interest is now tax exempt, permitting state and local taxpayers to borrow at subsidized rates.

Tax deductibility might seem to be an ideal way to give a slight open-ended price subsidy to state or local governments for all their public services, not unlike the ideal matching program shown in Figure 7.1. Letting t stand for the marginal federal income tax rate faced by a voter who itemizes deductions, deductibility effectively lowers the price of public services from P to P(1–t) for this voter, probably pretty close to P(1–m*) for most public services. But we should recognize three factors that complicate this neat solution to the externalities problem:

  • Tax rates are progressive, so rich voters get a bigger tax-induced subsidy than poor voters.
  • Since most low income taxpayers do not itemize deductions, they get no subsidy at all.
  • The fact that state or local public goods are provided at the sale level throughout the jurisdiction makes it particularly hard to tell who will benefit from the tax deduction.

The situation is described in Figure 7.2. Demand functions for local public services without externalities are shown for a typical rich itemizer (D_I) and a typical poor nonitemizer (D_N). The rich itemizer has a higher demand for public services but also faces a higher tax price because of his greater taxable income or property. For simplicity I assume these two differences are exactly offsetting, so both voters prefer quantity Q_0 without tax deductibility. Tax deductibility lowers the tax price of public services for the rich itemizer but not the poor nonitemizer.

If nonitemizers have a voting majority, as in the low-income community shown in the left panel, public spending will not change and tax deductibility is only a transfer from all federal taxpayers to rich itemizers. If itemizers have a voting majority, in the high-income community shown in the right panel, deductibility raises spending but is economically inefficient. The marginal valuation of public services is less than federal taxpayer cost for the rich, and less than local taxpayer cost for the poor. The subsidy does not look good either way. It subsidizes public spending in the rich but not the poor community—just the opposite of a power equalization grant.

One would, of course, want to study the matter more deeply because there could be all manner of combinations of voting majorities, initial desired spending levels, externalities, and patterns of price reductions. On a previous occasion I did try to work this all out, for a sample of Michigan voters with the tightening provisions implicit in the Tax Reform Act of 1986 (TRA) and with the assumption of full elimination of tax deductibility.[4] The results are shown in Table 7.4. A partial

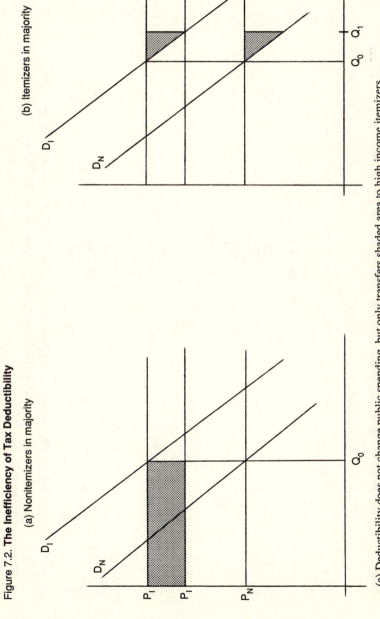

Figure 7.2. The Inefficiency of Tax Deductibility

(a) Nonitemizers in majority

(b) Itemizers in majority

(a) Deductibility does not change public spending, but only transfers shaded area to high income itemizers.
(b) Deductibility raises public spending to Q_1 and generates upper shaded triangle efficiency loss for each itemizer and lower shaded triangle efficiency loss for each nonitemizer.

Table 7.4

Desired Local Government Spending Under Different Tax Deductibility Provisions[a]

Place	Decrease			No Change	Increase			Sum
	>10	6–9	1–5		1–5	6–9	>10	
				1980 Tax Law[b]				
Detroit	7	5	2	*87*	3	27	18	149
Suburbs	20	16	9	*229*	3	30	25	332
Other	54	42	40	*428*	3	61	61	689
Total	81	63	51	*744*	9	118	104	1,170
				TRA of 1986[b]				
Detroit	23	6	15	*56*	8	26	15	149
Suburbs	65	26	81	*100*	21	27	12	332
Other	118	58	126	*265*	21	64	37	689
Total	206	90	222	*421*	50	117	64	1,170
				Full elimination[b]				
Detroit	37	14	6	*54*	4	21	13	149
Suburbs	165	32	14	*93*	3	17	8	332
Other	234	86	47	*250*	5	37	30	689
Total	436	132	67	*397*	12	75	51	1,170

Source: Edward M. Gramlich, "Federalism and Federal Deficit Reduction," *National Tax Journal 40* (September 1987), 299–313.

[a]Number of voters desiring specified changes in local spending and taxes, Michigan, 1978.

[b]Median voter class in italics.

elimination of tax deductibility, as was experienced under the TRA through the reduction in numbers of itemizers and the removal of the sales tax deduction, would be predicted to reduce public spending slightly in the high-income suburbs of Detroit and not at all elsewhere in the state. A full elimination would reduce public spending by up to 10 percent in those high-income suburbs of Detroit, slightly throughout the rest of the state, but not at all in the low-income city of Detroit. With these more detailed calculations, the subsidy still looks like perverse power equalization, and still transfers tax to high-income itemizers wherever they live. An obvious reform proposal is simply to eliminate income and property tax deductibility on the federal income tax.

The impact of the interest exemption is harder to predict because of what is known as the tax arbitrage problem. If state and local interest is not taxable, the state and local bond rate(s) will be bid down until marginal investors are indifferent between buying a taxable bond and earning $r(1-t)$ and buying a nontaxable bond and earning $s = r(1-t)$, where r is the market interest rate. It might seem that this reduction in the cost-of-capital would stimulate state and local borrowing and construction, and indeed it might to some extent. But in this era of sharp bond traders, there is another more likely impact. What is to stop local governments from borrowing at s, investing at r, pocketing the difference, and not changing capital construction at all? The Treasury has rules to limit this particular form of arbitrage, but other forms are possible, and exist in the real world.[5] The possibility of tax arbitrage makes it both inefficient and inequitable to open up differences in borrowing and lending rates such as is done by the tax exemption, and another obvious reform proposal is to eliminate the federal tax exemption of state and local interest.

Reform Proposals

This review of the present fiscal system has been motivated by a search for aspects that are inefficient and/or inequitable because they violate some basic canons of the theory of federalism. There are a number of aspects that fall into this category, which suggests several interesting policy changes. I now detail these suggestions in my own personal preference ordering, giving the rationale and, in Table 7.5, the likely improvement in the federal budget deficit in 1990 from making the change. That table also documents the source of any numbers that are used.

Table 7.5

Bold Fiscal Reform Plan, Fiscal Year 1990

Policy change	Federal deficit reduction (in billions of dollars)
Convert categorical grants	$5[a]
Eliminate tax deductibility	26[b]
Tax state and local interest	13[c]
Convert welfare grants	−9[d]
Net impact	$35

[a]Author's calculation.

[b]Congressional Budget Office, *Reducing the Deficit: Spending as Revenue Options* (March 1988) Option Rev.-15, p. 322.

[c]Edward M. Gramlich, "Federalism and Federal Deficit Reduction," *National Tax Journal* 40 (September 1987), 299–313.

[d]Edward M. Gramlich, "Cooperation and Competition in Public Welfare Policies," *Journal of Policy Analysis and Management* 6, no. 3 (Spring 1987), 417–31.

Convert Categorical Grants

The present matching grants do not achieve their goal of increasing spending in particular areas because the price subsidy is too generous on inframarginal units and not generous enough on marginal units. Roughly half of the grants listed in Table 7.3, those for transportation and sewage, could be converted to open-ended matching form with a price subsidy of about 0.3, roughly the level suggested by the pattern of internal and external benefits.[6] The federal budget saving would be about $5 billion in 1990, state citizens would lose a small amount, but there would be an economic efficiency gain of about $1 billion from the change.

While reductions in federal matching shares would seem to be logical policy changes in the face of pressures to reduce federal spending, there have as yet been very few such reductions. Most actual and proposed cuts are simply cuts in the amounts of grant-funded spending or consolidations of grants, both of which can be seen from Figure 7.1 to generate no improvements in economic efficiency. But there have been two recent movements in the direction of my proposal. The Omnibus Water Bill of 1986, for rivers, harbors, and other "pork barrel" type projects, requires state and local cost matching on new projects for the first time. The two Clean Water Acts passed in the 1980s have also reduced federal matching shares from 75 percent to a much lower figure by converting grants to a subsidized loan revolving fund.

Eliminate Tax Deductibility

The present deductibility of income and property taxes on the federal income tax is both inefficient and inequitable. It is inefficient because it subsidizes public spending unduly in some high-income communities. It is inequitable because it only goes to high-income taxpayers, whether they live in high- or low-income communities. The federal budget saving from completely eliminating deductibility would be enormous, $26 billion in 1990.

While a full elimination of tax deductibility has often been proposed, and was even included in the Treasury Department's initial tax reform proposal in 1985, steps in this direction so far have been very timid. State gasoline taxes were made nondeductible in the energy crisis of 1978 and sales taxes in the TRA of 1986. As was mentioned above, the cost of deductibility was further reduced in the TRA by the reduction in numbers of itemizers and the reduction in marginal income tax rates. Beyond this, there are various schemes to do part of the job: only let taxes be deducted at the bottom bracket rate, only let a share of taxes be deducted, only permit deduction of taxes in excess of some share of income. Any of these would be desirable changes, but the best change of all would be to eliminate tax deductibility altogether.

Tax Interest

The exclusion of state and local interest from federal taxable income drives down state and local bond rates. It might stimulate some capital construction, but its more likely effect is to open up arbitrage opportunities for state and local governments—they can borrow tax exempt and buy taxable bonds. The Internal Revenue Service does have rules against arbitrage, but there are lots of pairs of rates (r, $r(1-t)$, and s) that can be paired against each other and it is virtually impossible to police all forms of arbitrage. A good principle of tax administration is to keep arbitrage opportunities as low as possible, hence keeping the burden on the administrative enforcers as light as possible. This can be done by the simple expedient of taxing state and local interest, raising $13 billion in the process.

As with the other measures suggested, there have been some recent movements in this direction. By lowering marginal tax rates, the TRA reduced rate spreads on many forms of arbitrage. Moreover, the TRA contained some direct quantitative limits on arbitrage, limiting the amount of private-purpose bonds that could qualify for the interest exemption.

Convert AFDC Grants

One could make a strong case that the main welfare programs, Aid to Families with Dependent Children (AFDC) and Medicaid, should be straightforward national redistribution programs, just as is the federal personal income tax. Operating them at the state level, as is done now, leads to wide variations in state benefits and to unduly low average levels of benefits to the extent that state legislators are worried about the threat of migration (high benefits may attract welfare recipients to the state). These impacts are reduced by federal matching grants—which in this area are open-ended, with federal matching shares that range between 78 percent for low-income states and 50 percent for high-income states— and by the evening out that results from the national food stamps program. But benefit levels still vary widely across states, being roughly twice as high in high-benefit states as in low-benefit states.

It would be hard to revamp this system without a fundamental change, but there is a simpler way. There are efficiency reasons for having states bear some of the cost of Medicaid, in order to have an incentive to police costs. This program could be left as is. But there is no obvious sense in having states bear some of the cost of very low AFDC benefit levels. A simple reform would be to base federal matching shares not on state income, as now, but on benefit levels themselves. Federal matching ratios could be quite generous in those states that pay very low welfare benefits, just to bring these benefits up to decent levels. They could be quite strict, or indeed there could be no matching at all, in high-benefit states. Such a scheme would greatly reduce disparities in AFDC benefits around the country because it lowers the price most where the most reduction is needed.

To make a specific proposal, suppose federal matching shares for AFDC were raised to 100 percent for combined AFDC–food stamp benefits up to 60 percent of the poverty line; to 75 percent for benefits up to 80 percent of the poverty line; and to 50 percent up to the poverty line. Such a plan would raise living standards among welfare recipients by more than $3 billion in 1990, switch about $6 billion in welfare costs from states to the federal government, and cost the federal government about $9 billion in 1990.

For the first three policy reform proposals suggested, one can discern some recent movement in the direction of the proposal. In the case of AFDC, however, the drift is away from my proposal. The AFDC program actually had matching provisions along the lines I am proposing in its early days, from its first passage in the 1930s to the late 1960s. When the Medicaid program was added in the late 1960s, states were given the option of using the old kinked matching grant schedule or switching over to their Medicaid formula, which made matching rates constant for all benefit levels, at a rate determined by state relative income. In a sense, my proposal does nothing more than return to the old formulas for determining AFDC matching shares.

Higher Education Loans

At present, state governments pay large tuition subsidies to students to attend state supported universities. This scheme is arguably inefficient, both in subsidizing an activity where students probably can recapture most of their investment costs in subsequent income gains, and in distorting student college choices. It is also arguably inequitable, in that many low income taxpayers who do not benefit or have not benefited from higher education or higher education subsidies, subsidize the education of the middle and upper classes.

It is difficult to convert the subsidy to a loan program if it remains at the state level. The problem with states running life-cycle-type social insurance programs in this country is that interstate mobility is very high, necessitating complex tracking schemes. If states made higher education loans instead of grants, they would either have to collect on the graduate's income tax, in whatever state the graduate moves to, or on the graduate's loan. Experience with student loan repayment is already discouraging, and it would presumably become even more so if the university (to which the graduate might have some allegiance) is supplanted by some faraway state as the creditor.

The only way states can run nonsubsidy higher education plans is by a prepayment plan, examples of which are being studied in several states. In these, parents pay into a trust fund when children are very young and the savings accumulate into tuition credits when the child is ready for college. These credits will almost certainly be differential, implying distortion of choice, and there could be an incentive for the state to regulate the pricing and other policies of the university to make sure that prepaying parents' tuition credits can in fact pay the cost of higher education at the designated provider. Interstate mobility as the children are growing up could also present problems. These schemes are just now being adopted and perhaps will work well, but there are several potential inefficiencies.

If not the states, the national government. The national government can run an intertemporal trust fund, and a higher education loan program would be one such. The loans could in principle be repaid on either a debt- or an income-contingent basis: the issues here are complex and controversial, but they do not involve the federalism dimension. The only federalism point is that the national government seems best situated to conduct the type of higher education support program that seems most rational from an efficiency and equity standpoint.

In terms of details, one such plan, for loans ultimately supported by income-contingent payroll tax payments into a social insurance trust fund, was actually proposed by Michael Dukakis in the 1988 presidential campaign.[7] Were such a plan to be adopted, present federal subsidies to higher education running about $4 billion a year could either be dropped or devoted to grants to low income students. Beyond this, the true incremental budget cost of such a plan should be zero.

The latter claim concerns an important issue in budgetary accounting. On a cash basis, a postpayment plan would certainly entail budget outlays now and repayments later. But as the Congressional Budget Office has often argued, the cash budget is a very poor way to represent the government's financial position in the case of loans. These generally involve simple asset transfers, which leave both income and net worth unchanged for both the government and the private sector. In such cases a better representation can be gotten by recording the true subsidy, in a present value sense, whenever the government makes any credit transaction with the private sector. Were such accounting to be adopted for any nonsubsidized postpayment plan, the proper outlay entry would be zero, precisely what is entered in the federal deficit reduction in Table 7.5.

Summary

The U.S. system of fiscal federalism relationships conforms to the theoretical ideal reasonably well. With a few outstanding exceptions, public goods are by and large run by the governments that preside over their benefit area and social insurance funds are generally run at the national level. Taxes are redistributive at the national level and based more closely on benefits at the local level, as also conforms to the logic of federalism.

The outstanding exceptions concern income redistribution programs and higher education support, both of which seem inappropriately lodged at the state level. A programmatic remedy for the first anomaly is to alter the structure of welfare grants to lessen interstate benefit differences. Such a change would leave program operation at the state level but alter price incentives to narrow interstate differences in benefits and migration incentives. A programmatic remedy for the second anomaly is some form of a national loan program supported by a national trust fund.

There are other inefficiencies not involving the division of responsibilities but rather the structure of grants and tax incentives that benefit state and local citizens. The grant inefficiencies can be dealt with by reducing federal matching ratios but making grants open-ended. The tax inefficiencies can be dealt with by continuing the spirit of the TRA, under which tax preferences are eliminated so that marginal tax rates are kept as low as possible.

Were a package of such changes made, the federal deficit could be reduced by as much as $35 billion in 1990, 0.6 percent of GNP anticipated for that time or 20 percent of the deficit anticipated for that time. The reduction is not enormous, but not trivial either, and all the measures suggested improve both efficiency and equity.

Notes

1. The principle is described and defended by Wallace E. Oates, *Fiscal Federalism* (New York: Harcourt, Brace, Javanovich, Inc., 1972), chapter 2.
2. This issue is discussed in more detail in Edward M. Gramlich, "Reforming U.S. Fiscal Federalism Arrangements," in John M. Quigley and Daniel L. Rubinfeld, eds., 34–69, *American Domestic Priorities: An Economic Appraisal* (Berkeley: University of California Press, 1985).
3. This remedy was suggested by Ronald Coase, "The Problem of Social Cost," *Journal of Law and Economics* (October 1960).
4. Edward M. Gramlich, "Federalism and Federal Deficit Reduction," *Na-*

tional Tax Journal 40 (September 1987), 299–313.

5. See Roger H. Gordon and Joel Slemrod, ''An Empirical Examination of Municipal Financial Policy,'' in Harvey S. Rosen, ed., 53–78, *Studies in State and Local Public Finance* (Chicago: The University of Chicago Press, 1986).

6. Gramlich, ''Federalism and Federal Deficit Reduction,'' pp. 299–313.

7. The details are similar to that studied by Robert D. Reischauer, ''HELP: A Student Loan Program for the Twenty-first Century,'' in Lawrence E. Gladieux, ed., *Radical Reform or Incremental Change? Student Loan Policy Alternatives for the Federal Government* (New York: The College Board, 1988).

Index

State governments
  competitiveness among, 29–30, 80–81
  expenditure policy, 107–116
  federal aid to, 61–62, 98–105
  fiscal conditions, 105–107
  fiscal responsibility shifted to, 12, 83–84
  growth in, 57–59, 62–64
  local governments, aid to, 42–43, 73, 77–79, 113–14, 163
  neo-Progressive outlook, 48–50
  regional fiscal differences, 28–29, 64–73
  revenues, 31, 32, 34, 77–78, 91, 97
  tax policy, 89–98
Stockman, David, 10
Supplemental Security Income (SSI), 110, 112
Supreme Court, U.S., 19–20
Surplus, 74–76

Tax Reform Act of 1988 (TRA), 164, 167, 170
Taxes
  1986 reform, 77–81, 132–33
  arbitrage, 167, 169–70
  centralization of powers, 65, 66
  city revenues, 43, 128–29, 130–31, 138–39
  corporate, 20, 93
  cuts, 27, 30
  deductibility, 163–67, 169
  distribution by levels of government, 158–59
  federal, increased, 82
  federal off-budget expenditures, 44–46, 51
  income, individual, 20, 25–26, 34, 93
  interest exempt from, 163, 167, 169–70

Taxes *(continued)*
  local, increased, 59
  mobilization, 65–66
  property tax, 9, 13, 71, 78, 92
  regional differences, 28–29
  sales, 34, 93, 120
  severance, 96
  state, increased, 12–13, 59, 120
  state policy, 89–98
  subsidies, 163–67
  value added, 119–20

Technology, state promotion of, 51–52
TRA. *See* Tax Reform Act of 1988

Urban areas
  civil rights, 38
  crime rate, 140
  federal government policies toward, 37–43, 129–30, 132–33
  financial management, 133–38
  fiscal health, 142–48
  future prospects, 50–52, 148
  municipal bonds, 131–32, 136–37
  neighborhood policy, 44–46
  pension plans, 134
  poor, tax reform's effect upon, 81
  public choice theory, 40
  public services, 139–141
  revenues, 43, 128–29, 130–31, 138–39
  short term debt, 134–35
  state aid, 42–43

Value added tax. *See* Taxes, value added

Wartime. *See* Defense spending
Welfare, public. *See* Social welfare; specific programs

Contributors

ROY W. BAHL, JR. is a professor of economics and the director of the Policy Research Program at Georgia State University. He has served as Maxwell Professor of Economics and the director of the Metropolitan Studies Program in the Maxwell School–Syracuse University, a visiting scholar with the World Bank, a fellow of the East-West Center, and as an economist with the Fiscal Affairs Department of the International Monetary Fund. Since earning his Ph.D. from the University of Kentucky in 1965 and a B.A. from Greenville College in 1961, he has published more than one hundred professional articles, fifteen monographs, and twelve books. His latest book, coauthored with Johannes F. Linn, is entitled *Urban Public Finance in Developing Countries*. Dr. Bahl also has served on the editorial boards of five major professional journals and on the Board of Directors of the National Tax Association/Tax Institute of America (which he also served as president), the Lincoln Foundation, and the New York State Energy Research and Development Authority. He has been a consultant or the project director of more than eighty domestic and international studies dealing with state and local government finance. He has received the Chancellor's Citation at Syracuse University and the Pioneer Medal from the Republic of the Philippines.

STEVEN D. GOLD is the director of fiscal studies for the National Conference of State Legislatures and is the director of the Fiscal Federalism Project funded by the Ford Foundation. Prior to joining NCSL in 1981, he served as a professor of economics at Drake University, where he was on the faculty for nine years. He received his Ph.D. from the University of Michigan and B.A. from Bucknell University. He has functioned as an editor on the boards of three major journals, including the *National Tax Journal*, and on the Board of Directors of the American Education Finance Association. He has published numerous professional articles and has written or edited ten books, the most recent of which is *The Unfinished Agenda for State Tax Reform*.

EDWARD M. GRAMLICH is currently a professor of economics and public policy at the University of Michigan where he was the chairman of the Department of Economics and the director of the Institute of Public

Policy Studies. In 1986 and 1987 he was deputy director and acting director of the Congressional Budget Office and in the early 1970s was a senior fellow of the Brookings Institution and director of the Policy Research Division for the Office of Economic Opportunity. He earned his Bachelor's Degree from Williams College and his M.A. and Ph.D. from Yale University. He has served on the editorial boards of four major professional journals, has published eight books, and written more than sixty journal articles and chapters of books.

RICHARD CHILD HILL has held an academic position at Michigan State University since 1971 and is currently a professor of sociology and urban affairs. He graduated from the University of California, Berkeley with a B.A. in 1966 and earned his M.S. and Ph.D. degrees at the University of Wisconsin. He has coauthored two books—*Detroit: Race and Uneven Development* and *Restructuring the City: The Political Economy of Urban Redevelopment*—and written more than fifty professional articles.

HELEN F. LADD has been a professor of public policy studies at Duke University since 1986. She has also taught at Dartmouth College, Wellesley College, and at Harvard University. She graduated with a B.A. from Wellesley College in 1967, received a Master's Degree from the London School of Economics in 1968, and earned her Ph.D. in economics from Harvard University in 1974. An expert on state and local public finance, she has written extensively on the property tax, education finance, tax and expenditure limitations, intergovernmental aid, state economic development, and the fiscal problems of U.S. cities. Her most recent book (with John Yinger) is *America's Ailing Cities: Fiscal Health and the Design of Urban Policy*. She is on the Policy Council of the Association for Public Policy and Management, on the editorial boards of several journals, and has consulted on tax policy and intergovernmental relations for all three branches of government. She has been a Visiting Scholar at the Federal Reserve Bank of Boston for the past three summers, and during 1989–90, is a senior Research Fellow at the Lincoln Institute for Land Policy in Cambridge, Massachusetts.

JOHN E. PECK is professor of economics at Indiana University at South Bend, where he also serves as director of the South Bend campus's Bureau of Business and Economic Research. He earned his Bachelor's Degree from the University of Notre Dame and holds an M.B.A. from Michigan State University and a Ph.D. in economics from the University of Notre Dame. He has been a recipient of several Distinguished Teaching Awards, a Lilly Endowment Faculty Fellowship, and a Lundquist Faculty Fellow award. He is a past president of the Michiana Chapter, National Association of Business Economists. Dr. Peck has published more than thirty articles and monographs on subjects that include the financing of the nation's public elementary and secondary schools, Indiana's taxing and expenditure system, and the evolving structure of the South Bend economy.

JOHN SHANNON is now a senior fellow at The Urban Institute. Prior to joining The Urban Institute, he served on the staff of the Advisory Commission on Intergovernmental Relations for twenty-four years—first as senior analyst, then as assistant director of the Public Finance Staff, and most recently as executive director. He has also served at the local level with the Detroit Bureau of Governmental Research, at the state level with the Kentucky Department of Revenue, and at the federal level on the White House staff. Dr. Shannon's academic background is in the field of public finance and political science, and he has taught political science courses at Creighton University in Omaha, George Washington University in Washington, DC, and lectured at the Centre for Federalism at the University of Australia. He has published over a hundred articles in public and intergovernmental finance. He graduated from the University of Notre Dame (B.A.), Wayne State University (M.P.A.), and the University of Kentucky (Ph.D.). In 1988, he received the Donald C. Stone Award for significant contributions in the Intergovernmental Research Area from the American Society for Public Administration.

THOMAS R. SWARTZ is a professor of economics and the college fellow for the College of Arts and Letters at the University of Notre Dame. He came to South Bend in 1965 after completing degrees at Indiana (—Ph.D. 1965), Ohio (—M.A. 1962), and LaSalle (—B.A. 1960). He has served as a fiscal consultant with federal agencies, the State of Indiana, and a number of local governments. He has authored, coauthored, or coedited four books, three monographs, and more than twenty-five chapters of books or professional articles, and has delivered more than thirty papers here and abroad. The fifth edition of *Taking Sides*, coedited with Frank J. Bonello, will be published in 1990.